YOU CAN SELL

Shiv Khera is the founder of **Qualified Learning Systems Inc., USA.** An author, educator, business consultant and successful entrepreneur, he is a much sought-after speaker.

He inspires and informs people, helping them to realize their true potential. He has taken his dynamic personal messages to opposite sides of the globe, from the U.S. to Singapore. His 30 years of research, understanding and experience has helped people achieve personal growth and fulfillment.

He has been recognized as a **'Louis Marchesi Fellow'** by **the Round Table Foundation,** an award given to, among others, **Mother Teresa. Lions Club International** has honored him with **'Lifetime Achievement Award'** for the cause of **'Humanitarian Service to Society'.** The **Rotary Club** has honored him with the **'Centennial Vocational Award for Excellence'.**

Shiv Khera's client list includes, among others, **Lufthansa, Johnson & Johnson, Motorola, Nestle, GSK, Tetrapak, Phillips, Gillette, HSBC, Carrier, IBM, Ericsson** and **GM.** He has appeared on numerous radio and television shows.

Tens of thousands have benefitted from his **dynamic workshops** in 17 countries and millions have heard him as a keynote speaker.

Shiv Khera is the author of 12 books including the **international bestseller** *You Can Win,* which has sold over **1.7 million copies** in 16 languages. His other books are on the way to creating new records.

His trademark is:

> **'Winners don't do different things.**
> **They do things differently.'®**

YOU CAN SELL

RESULTS ARE REWARDED
EFFORTS AREN'T

SHIV KHERA

Rupa & Co

Copyright © Shiv Khera 2010

First Published 2010
Seventh Impression 2011

Published by
Rupa Publications India Pvt. Ltd.
7/16, Ansari Road, Daryaganj,
New Delhi 110 002

Sales Centres:

Allahabad Bengaluru Chennai
Hyderabad Jaipur Kathmandu
Kolkata Mumbai

Photo credit: Hari Krishna Katragadda

Typeset by
Mindways Design
1410 Chiranjiv Tower
43 Nehru Place
New Delhi 110 019

Printed in India by
Rekha Printers Pvt. Ltd.
A-102/1, Okhla Industrial Area, Phase-II,
New Delhi-110 020

This book is dedicated to those professionals
who bring pride to the profession
through ethical selling.
To them,
the sky is not the limit.

CONTENTS

PREFACE

So long as you have your eyes on the goal, you don't see obstacles.

Unless there is a change in behavior, learning does not take place. Transformation only takes place when information is internalized. Most people fail in life not because they lack talent but because they lack the burning desire.

You must have heard many self-made success stories, but have you ever heard of a self-made failure story? Probably not! Why? It's because failures never accept responsibility. They will blame their parents, teachers, the economy, the stars, luck, their horoscope, or whatever.

What Kind of Book is This?

In one sense, it is a cookbook. It lists the ingredients—the principles—you will need to follow to become successful, and gives you the recipe for mixing them in the correct proportions.

Above all, this is a guidebook – a step-by-step, 'How–to' book that can help you turn dreams into realities.

How to Read this Book

You Can Sell will help you establish new goals, develop a new sense of purpose, and generate new ideas about yourself and your future.

The concepts in this book cannot be absorbed by casual browsing or in one reading. It should be read slowly and carefully, one chapter at a time. Don't move on to the next chapter until you are sure you understand every concept in the previous chapter.

Use this as a workbook. Write marginal notes for yourself. Use a highlighter as you read and mark those words or sentences or paragraphs that seem vital, or especially applicable to you.

As you read, discuss the concepts in each chapter with your spouse or partner, or with a close friend. A second (and hopefully frank) opinion from someone who knows your strengths and weaknesses can be especially helpful.

Start an Action Plan

One of the purposes of this book is to help you create an Action Plan for the rest of your life. If you have never created an Action Plan, it defines three things:

1. What you want to achieve
2. How you expect to achieve it
3. When you plan to achieve it

As you read this book, keep a notebook handy. Divide it into three sections – your goals, the stages in which you plan to reach them, and your timetable for success.

By the time you finish reading this book, your notebook will be the foundation on which you can build your new life.

The principles in this book are universal. They are applicable in any situation, organization, or country. As Plato said, 'Truths are eternal.'

Throughout the book I have used the masculine gender, only for the purpose of ease in writing. The principles apply to both genders.

ACKNOWLEDGEMENTS

I want to recognize the support of my wife, my son-in-law and my staff, whose diligent efforts have made this book possible.

This book is an essence of my personal selling experience and the learning and training provided to me by my teachers, mentors, and thought leaders who have inspired me. I am sharing knowledge which I have internalized during my 35 years of experience in the field of selling. I have learned from many people, much wiser than me, and a lot of other sources. Even though it is not possible to give credit to each one separately, I am deeply indebted to all.

I wish to express my gratitude to those who may have contributed to this work directly or indirectly even though they remain anonymous.

1

WHO IS NOT SELLING?

Aren't We All Selling?

- A candidate at a job interview. The candidate is selling his candidature and the interviewer is selling his company.
- A boy and girl proposing to get married.
- A politician making speeches to get votes.
- A lawyer arguing his client's case in court.
- A government body negotiating a major contract.

Aren't They All selling?

Our selling ability determines the success or failure of any transaction. At seminars I ask my audience '*How many people are in direct selling?*' Very few hands go up. When I ask those who have not raised their hands what profession are they in, then they say: 'I am a doctor/computer engineer/an accountant,' etc. I share with them the definition of a salesperson as given by Robert Stevenson. He said *'Anyone who sells a product, service or an idea is a sales person.'* Based on this definition, who is not selling? A mother sells her ideas to a child, doesn't she? The consideration is not monetary but emotional.

We are always selling either for or against ourselves. The way we talk, walk, dress, meet and greet others says something about us. Our overall personality either leaves a favorable or unfavorable impression on others. Everyone in every company is constantly selling either for or against the company. For example, the way the telephone operator answers the phone, her/his tone either says – *'I am glad you called'* or *'you are bothering me.'*

Selling is a Win-Win or Lose-Lose Game

When a sale is complete and we have sold a solution to someone, it means we have helped them get rid of some pain or achieve some gain. If either of these 2 things hasn't happened, then we are doing a disservice. The buyer is deprived of a gain or continues bearing his pain, and both the seller and buyer have lost the time forever. The seller has also lost an opportunity to provide a solution elsewhere. Imagine if something could be of benefit to someone and you don't provide that benefit for an investment. In that case, both of you are losing. This is called *lose-lose.* The seller has lost his time forever and the potential source of revenue, and the buyer has been deprived of a solution.

By completing the transaction, both parties gain – the buyer by purchasing the solution, and seller by getting paid for serving the buyer.

When a seller sells the solution, it is called *win-win*, because both parties end up gaining.

The way I see it, Marketing strategizes the sources of revenue, but it is Sales that actually bring in the revenue

Selling is considered to be a function of marketing. When sales results are good, marketing takes credit. When the sales are bad, the sales department and sales people are blamed.

Why has Selling become a bigger challenge today than it was yesterday?

1. Today a buyer has many more options.
2. Competition has also become sophisticated.
3. Media has made people more knowledgeable and aware.
4. There is a terminology called 'Caveat Emptor' which means 'Buyer Beware'. That is the old thinking. Today the scenario is 'Seller Beware'. Why 'seller beware'? This is because the seller is perceived as an expert in his field. The buyer who may or may not be knowledgeable in this area is relying on the seller's trustworthiness. Today the buyer is relying on the seller's character and competence to sell him the right product. This is where the seller's integrity is put to test.

People often complain of competition. The way I see it, if you had no competition how could anyone rate or grade you? When you have competition, if you are good, you look better and if you are bad, you look worse because people have something or someone to compare you with.

Success in selling really demonstrates the survival of the fittest. Fitness is the professionalism in a sales professional, which is a learnt trait. Isn't it a small premium to pay for a great life?

The profession of selling really is the domain of the elite. The elite professional is like the cream that rises to the top, no matter how big or small the container.

Aren't you self-employed? If not, who are you working for?

All sales professionals are self-employed entrepreneurs and unless they consider themselves self-employed they will not succeed. The real question is – if you are not working for yourself then who are you working for? In a free economy nothing happens unless a sale takes place. A sales professional moves products and services from the producer to the end user. He keeps the wheels of the economy moving and helps generate income thus playing a very important role in the economy. In fact, without the profession of selling one wonders what would happen to the national or international economy? Hence, a robust economy strongly depends on good salesmanship. Many countries have thousands and some millions of sales people. *Just imagine if each salesperson in each company made 1 extra sale per year or even better in a month, what would happen to the national economy!* It would shoot up!!

It is a Learnt Profession

Every profession needs specialization. An architect cannot perform brain surgery. A medical doctor cannot represent you in a law suit. A lawyer cannot construct a building. Today, more college graduates are taking up the profession of selling than ever before. In fact, I heard a professor say that over 50% of college graduates are going in to the profession of selling after completing their formal education. The demand for good sales professionals is high but the supply is very low, resulting in a big gap. Doctors have to go through medical school, engineers have to go to engineering college but rarely do you find a professional education program for sales people. A good fundamental sales curriculum is missing. Thus good, effective sales people are hard to find.

Anyone can learn the art of selling and excel in this great profession. The problem is not that people cannot learn the art of selling; the reality is they lack the attitude to learn. Most people fail in life not because they lack talent, but because they lack the burning desire.

Learning to sell is like learning to ride a bicycle. Remember the first time when we were learning to ride a bicycle. Most likely, we started with the bicycle that had training wheels attached on both sides. If you recall the first experience, it was rather scary. We were afraid to fall and get hurt, and our objective was to learn eventually to ride without training wheels. As we stumbled when something went wrong, the training wheels protected us till we became proficient enough to balance on 2 wheels and ride effortlessly.

Just analyze the learning process. It was the process, persistence and practice that brought the proficiency. The exact same thing is true in learning to sell. Just like you cannot learn to swim by reading a book, similarly the profession of selling cannot just be learned or taught unless it is practiced on the ground.

This book not only shares with you what to do but also how to do it. This book does not contain theoretical knowledge but contains practical ideas that work and can bring positive results. In this book, we shall discuss time-tested, proven principles which make a good professional salesperson. The word I use is '**principles**' not '**tactics**'. This is because tactics are manipulative, whereas, principles have their foundation on the following 3 values:

+ **Integrity**
+ **Respect**
+ **Responsibility**

In order for this book to benefit you and show results, it must be read carefully, completely and then internalized. Reading without internalizing will not help. Just as an athlete builds stamina by constant practice similarly a good sales professional builds proficiency with regular practice. My suggestion to you is don't just read this book, but underline practical ideas and personalize them. They are ready to use and will help lead you towards lasting success. Whether you are new in the field of selling or a veteran, these ideas bring fresh perspectives.

The best part of success is it starts with you, it starts now and it starts here!!

2

A CHOSEN PROFESSION

Many times, I have been asked that if I had a rewind button in my life and if I could relive my life again, which profession would I pick. Would I be a doctor, an engineer, an attorney or an accountant? My answer is '*I have respect for all these professions, but the only profession that I will pick, and pick much earlier in my life, would be that of a commission salesman, not a salaried salesman.*' The reason for this is that a salesman on commission writes his own pay cheque. He decides his own compensation. He says '*Pay me nothing if I do not produce!*' The best part of selling is that a good sales professional controls and in fact, creates his own destiny. Good sales professionals are goal driven. They realize that in life results are rewarded, not efforts. In cricket, no matter how many times a batsman scores 99 runs, nobody ever gives a grace run to call it a century!

The world only rewards results, not efforts.

The Start of My Career in Selling

It is not unusual to see many people enter the profession of selling totally by accident. I am such an example.

My career started in the USA. Once, I saw an advertisement in the newspaper saying, '*If you want to make some extra money do door-to-door demonstrations of vacuum cleaners.*' I responded to the advertisement. I thought, 'During the day I will wash cars and in the evening I would do the demos.' There were a lot of people there. We got a pep talk and were told '*go do the demos of the vacuum cleaner. For every demo you do, you will get paid 5 dollars.*' I was genuinely naïve and actually believed that I only had to do the demo and not to sell. I would go to an apartment building, knock on the door and when the lady or man opened the door, I would say, '*Madam/Sir, you don't have to buy the vacuum cleaner, all that you have to do is take a demo and I will get 5 dollars.*' Some people took pity on me and let me come in, some people slammed the door, but that was all right. One day I was doing a demo at an Indian family's home. The husband and wife were sitting

The world only rewards results, not efforts.

on the sofa and I was on the floor. The entire time, the man instead of looking at the vacuum cleaner, kept looking at me. I asked, '*Sir, did I do something wrong?*'

He said, '*No.*'

I asked, '*Why do you look at me this way?*'

He asked me, '*Shiv, have you ever sold life insurance?*'

I said, *'Never, and I never will, because I remember, back home the life insurance agent was the pest who would not leave me alone for 3 hours till I signed the application. I will never be that pest in my life'.*

He said, *'No Shiv, it doesn't work that way here. Look at me, I am a life insurance agent. Look at my lifestyle, I drive a Lincoln car.'* Later on I came to know that he was working for MetLife, and the manager was having a recruitment drive going on. If you recruited a new salesperson, you would get a Samsonite briefcase. So, to him I was the briefcase!

I said, *'Thank you, but no thank you.'* I finished the demo and left.

When in life you cannot go straight, you go the other way around. We were living in the same building; his wife became friendly with my wife and somehow she convinced her that selling life insurance was the right thing to do. My wife also knew that we had to do something different; we couldn't go through life washing cars. I had a family to support. We had a little daughter and my wife knew that it would not be easy for her to convince me either.

She knew how to handle the situation well. She said, *'Shiv, to sell life insurance you have to take an exam. Why don't you take the exam and if you pass, you have a choice. Right now, you have no choice.'*

I said, *'OK, I will take the exam, but I won't sell.'* I took the exam and passed. So this person, who had gotten the whole process started, asked me to come along to his office and meet the District Manager. The District Manager was a very sharp, mature person by the name of Joe Bonny, who congratulated me and said, '*Shiv, if you decide to sell life insurance right now, I will make you an offer and I will give you time to think.*' Then, he pulled out his watch, and said '*If you become an agent right now, I shall give you a draw of $150 a week and you have 30 seconds to decide before I withdraw the offer.*'

I said, '*Joe, you said you will give me time to think.*'

He nodded and said, '*You have 20 seconds left.*'

I said, '*I will take it.*' Now I was a life insurance agent, something I never wanted to be! I was given the rate book, some training and they said, '*Boy, go and sell!*'

For the next 3 months I went out selling and I thought I was putting in a 100% effort. We all have our own perceptions of hard work. I broke the company's record. Guess, how many sales I made? Almost none! My manager called me and said, '*I have been in the life insurance business for close to 35 years and I have seen some slow starts in my life, but I have never seen one like you. Don't come back tomorrow, you are fired.*'

I said, '*Joe, at least hear me out before you fire me. I am not a doctor, an engineer or an accountant. I am only a B.Com and I failed in my 10th grade. I'm not an educated person. I have a handicap. How do you expect performance out of me?*' That day, somebody spoke very harshly to me, and I am glad he did, because that was not anger, it was concern.

Joe said, '*You shut up and listen to me today. You don't have a handicap, you have a bad attitude. It is people like you who ruin not only their own life, but their family's life, too. Do you know who has a handicap? It's the doctor, engineer, attorney and accountant.*' I had never heard that before.

I asked, '*How do they have a handicap?*'

He said, *'Go check out all over the world. It is generally true (exceptions are different) that they have all picked their fields and they are stuck. You have not picked your field. Don't you see the world is open to you? In fact, the world is waiting for you!'*

I said, *'Joe, I never thought from that point of view.'*

He said, *'Now that you are fired, you have all the time to think. Please leave my office.'*

I left the office very depressed and dejected. That night I had an appointment about 30 miles away and I wanted to keep it, because all our appointments were made 1 week in advance.

It was around 6.30 in the evening, and while I was driving I was feeling very low and depressed. I knew that I had no job the next day. In my bout of depression, involuntarily, I just started crying. I had a family to support, and didn't know how to earn a living. I had a little daughter and I didn't know how to put bread on the table for the family. I kept crying and I kept praying. Finally, half an hour later, I reached the venue of my appointment, got myself composed, went up and started selling. I got in at about 7 p.m. and started my presentation. By the time the man looked at his watch it was 11.30 at night. No wonder life insurance agents are called pests. The client said to me, *'Do you realize what time it is?'* I got the message that this was his polite way of saying 'get out'. Then he said, *'Do you realize that I have to go to work tomorrow morning?'*

I said, *'I am sure you do, Sir'*. This was another polite way of saying get out now. But somehow I was not moving that night. I don't know what got into this person's mind. He said *'Tell me, what will it cost me to get rid of you right now.'*

I thought he was asking me the rate. I opened the book, flipped through the pages, came to his age, looked at the factor, multiplied with the amount of insurance and I said, *'Sir, that will be $27.58 cents (to the best of my recollection)'.*

He said, *'Is that all? Why didn't you tell me that when you walked in?'* He wrote me a cheque and said, *'Take this and go.'*

I said, *'Sir, will you please sign the application, too?'* That was my first sale! I came home at midnight and the next morning I went to my manager and said, *'Joe, I have an application today. It is a **small** one but it is a bound one* (a bound one is one with a cheque, because an application without a cheque is also without a commitment!). *Joe, will you let me stay? Could you withdraw the papers to fire me, because if you fire me, I don't know where to go? The only place I know where to go is to go back to washing cars and I don't want to do it anymore. I make a commitment to you that I will not let you down. Please withdraw the papers.'*

He looked at me and said, *'Shiv, this is not your small one. This is your **big** one and I will only let you stay here if you make a commitment, not to me but, to yourself and your family. I will withdraw the papers.'* That day, I made a commitment to myself and that was a major turning point in my life. He withdrew the papers and let me stay. That year, I went ahead and sold close to $1 million worth of life insurance. The next year, I sold close to $3 million dollars (including term insurance). The same year, I came to know from my manager that I had missed achieving the MDRT (qualifying for the select Million Dollar Round Table) status. The year after, I sold enough to qualify for and achieve the MDRT status.

After I moved to the USA, I got into 3 businesses, and bought out a pension and contract administration franchise (around early 80s). My wife and I started an office in New Jersey with no clients and finally sold our practice in the mid-90s with close to 400 clients.

Why Do I Share My Life Story with You?

1. The major reason – when my manager said, *'You shut up and listen to me!'*, he got my attention. That was the time I learnt a very important lesson– **'Sometimes in life you've got to be unkind to be kind'.** Leadership is not a popularity contest. He spoke to me as a parent and as a teacher. What a message!

2. All my life I kept failing and blaming the whole world for my failure, not realizing that I was my biggest problem. Nothing changed outside, but something changed inside me and gave me a new direction in life. Many times in life **aren't we our own biggest problem**? That's the time I learnt that selling is more a matter of will than skill and we need both. Between will and skill, will is more important than skill. Skill can be matched, but when you are down and hurt, that's the time when your sheer **will** is going to pull you up one more time, to get up and make one more call and that is the winning edge. Even though it has become a cliché, it still makes great sense. The difference between the ordinary and extraordinary is only the 'extra'.

> **Selling is more a matter of will than skill and we need both.**

3. At my seminars I ask participants, '*How many have been to the horse races?*' Invariably hands go up. The winning horse that comes first, wins 3 to one, 5 to 1 or 10 to 1, depending on the odds. The question is whether the horse that wins ten to 1 is 10 times faster than the one behind him? The answer is no. The winning horse may only be faster by the nose, but the rewards are 10 times bigger. Is it fair? Who cares? What difference does it make? Those are the rules of the game. Whatever happens at the horse races is exactly true in our human life, too. The question is – do we have to be 10 times smarter than our competition? The answer is no. All we need is the nose and the rewards are 10 times bigger in real life too. The difference between winning and losing, many times, is very little. At the Olympics, the gold-medal winner beats those behind him by probably a fraction of a second. Michael Phelps created a world record by winning 8 gold medals at the 2008 Olympics in Beijing, China. He won the 100-meter butterfly race by $1/100^{th}$ of a second. An elite sales professional is like a race horse with the winner's edge and the athlete who wins by a fraction of a second, but is rewarded 10 times more.

An elite sales professional is like a race horse with the winner's edge and the athlete who wins by a fraction of a second, but is rewarded 10 times more.

3

PRIDE IN THE PROFESSION OF SELLING

Image of an Average Salesperson

Sometimes, negative perceptions develop towards certain professions given the behavior of some individuals. Many people consider a salesperson as a fast talking conman who will sell his soul to make a quick buck. They are only interested in commissions at any cost. They want to make a sale by hook or by crook. Many times, you hear people saying that to succeed you need to learn the 'tricks of the trade'. Cheats and crooks learn the tricks; a good professional only learns the trade.

Selling with integrity is a noble profession. To most people selling is an occupation but to the career-minded, it is a great profession. I have learnt one thing in my career – a good sales professional will always have a job and a great sales professional will make an above average income. I feel very strongly that selling is the highest-paying profession in the world.

When I decided to go into the profession of selling some of my friends said, 'Why don't you get a proper job?' That was almost 35 years ago. Today, I am proud of the noble profession of selling and to be a part of it. I feel great pride in being called a sales professional first, and thereafter an author.

It is the competence and proficiency of the professional that determines his potential. It is the character of the practitioner that brings goodwill or ill-will to both him and the profession.

Why do you go to a doctor 10 miles away, bypassing many other doctors on the way? Is he the most qualified? Probably not. Why do you go to a mechanic 10 miles away to get your car repaired, bypassing many other mechanics on the way? Is he the most qualified? Probably not! Something tells you that you are dealing with the right person. What is that 'something'? That 'something' is called the 'I' factor. What is the 'I' factor? 'I' factor is the intuition or gut feeling. It is always the intangible spark, which connects us together.

Supposing you were offered a product, identical in price and other terms and conditions, by two parties who would you buy from? The answer is obvious; if all other things are equal, it is the comfort level with the sales person which will determine who you buy from. What is comfort level? It is the unsaid emotional feeling of ease.

People buy more from the heart rather than the head. A good sales professional not only makes a presentation but he sells himself, his product and his company and in that order.

Even if there is a good product from a good company but the prospect is not comfortable with the sales person, he will not buy.

Selling is as much an inner game as an outer game. Our inner commitment, belief, pride in performance, integrity and persistence, are all reflected in our performance outside.

The selling profession offers many challenges but also many rewards for those who succeed. For a good salesperson, it can mean a lifetime of prosperity and security for himself and his family. The opportunities and rewards for a professional salesperson are unlimited. As a sales professional what are your rewards in life?

There are two kinds of rewards for every sales professional – internal and external.

Internal Rewards are Intrinsic – they are intangible or invisible and can only be felt. Intrinsic rewards only come when the salesperson's actions are driven by positive values and attitude. They include:

1. Gratification
2. Satisfaction
3. Fulfillment
4. Meaningfulness
5. Peace of mind
6. Happiness
7. Security
8. Confidence

External Rewards Are Extrinsic – they are tangible and visible. Extrinsic rewards are driven by ambition, goals, and hard work. The financial rewards are important. However, if they are not value-driven, then one may make money but have no fulfillment and other intrinsic rewards. External rewards include:

1. Monetary rewards (wealth)
2. Recognition
3. Respect
4. Prestige
5. Good life
6. Comfort

A good sales professional can have a great income and a fulfilling career, regardless of his products or company.

What is Selling?

Selling is nothing but the **transfer of enthusiasm** from the seller to the buyer. Supposing you became as enthusiastic about my product as I am, you would end up buying it, wouldn't you? If I am not enthusiastic about my own product, I have no right to sell it. Which means, if I am not passionate about my own product, why should anyone else be? How can I sell it? Do I have a right to sell it?

A salesperson while selling grocery was referring to everything he sold as one, 2 or 3 pounds of enthusiasm etc. The buyer asked *'When I buy 2 pounds of carrots why do you refer to it as 2 pounds of enthusiasm?'* The salesperson replied,

'Whenever anyone buys anything from the store I always put in 200% of enthusiasm behind it.'

What this illustrates is that a good salesperson should have a strong belief in his product. Strong belief means that under the same set of circumstances, if the salesperson would not buy his own product, he certainly has no right to sell it to anyone. If under the same circumstances, a doctor would not prescribe a medicine to his own children, he has no right to prescribe it to other people. If he does, he is cheating people. If you sell something that you don't believe in:

1. You are not a good professional
2. You are cheating people
3. People sense it instinctively and get a feeling of discomfort.

Selling is 90% conviction and 10% Communication of the Conviction

I recall, when I joined Metropolitan Life Insurance at the beginning of my sales career, I used to sell small policies of face values of $5,000 or $10,000. My average policies were of $10,000. I used to hear the top producers in the industry talking of making big sales. Once I was talking to one such professional and he said, *'You can never convince a client to buy a million dollar policy unless you own one. Supposing you died, how much insurance would your family need for food, clothing, shelter, children's education, etc. in order to survive?'*

I answered *'A million dollars.'*

He asked me – *'Then why don't you own a million dollar policy yourself? If you don't own it yourself, you have no right to sell it to anyone, because you have no conviction.'* It took me several months to convince myself, but the day I bought my own policy, I started selling policies of face values of $500,000 to $1 million with as much comfort and ease as I used to sell $10,000 policies.

Success is not measured by how we do as compared to others, but how we do as compared to what we are capable of doing. Winners compete against themselves; they better their own records constantly.

Pride in performance and the profession of selling can only come when we internalize and merge **character** and **competence** together, to create something called a great sales professional. For that we need to understand the principles of selling and the process involved. They are as follows:

1. Commitment to be a good sales professional
2. Focus on goals
3. Acquiring competencies in selling skills
4. Creating and following a selling system
5. Putting in an organized effort
6. Giving and getting respect
7. Learning to relate to people
8. Lead generation and prospecting
9. Qualifying prospects
10. Learning to approach to build rapport

Winners compete against themselves; they better their own records constantly.

11. Building trust
12. Identifying the decision-making process and key decision-makers
13. Fact-finding and making presentations
14. Learning to ask questions to direct the sales call
15. Uncovering the need of the customer
16. Providing solutions
17. Overcoming resistance
18. Closing a sale
19. Keeping post-sales commitments and service
20. Building the post-sale relationship
21. Avoiding mistakes and learning from experience
22. Learning how to stay motivated and how to handle rejections

All of the above can be classified into 3 distinct activities – the pre-sale, the actual sale and the post-sale – and all are necessary in order to be a good professional.

Are Sales People Born or Made?

The mistaken belief is that one needs no qualification, or talents to make a success in the profession of selling. The fact is that selling skills are acquired even by great professionals. None of us are born with them.

In some countries that I have travelled to, I have picked up the morning newspaper to find an announcement of the birth of a baby girl or a baby boy. In the same newspaper, the obituary column carries an announcement that so and so person died, he was an eminent lawyer, doctor, etc. If you notice by birth, no one is a salesperson, an accountant, an attorney, or a doctor; they are only a boy or a girl. But upon death he/she died as an eminent professional. That means that somewhere between birth and death by training, education or practice they became eminent, elite professionals.

4

ATTITUDE DETERMINES SUCCESS

A Positive Attitude Determines Success

Sales depend more upon the attitude of the sales professional than that of the prospect. A good sales professional is never ashamed of his profession. In fact, he is proud of his profession. The only thing he is ashamed of is non-performance.

There is a very commonly used story by many sales managers – two salesmen went to Africa, both went to sell shoes in different parts of the same country. They both saw villagers without shoes. One immediately sent a message back to his manager saying *'There is no market here. Nobody wears shoes and hence I am coming back.'*

The other sent a message saying, *'Get ready for big sales – there is a huge market here. Nobody wears shoes and we can make everyone wear them. Gear up production.'*

The difference is the attitude.

Vacuum Cleaner Salesman in a Snowstorm

Winners turn a negative into a positive. Winners do it in spite of problems, not in absence of, and losers permanently rationalize and make excuses in life.

Most people who call themselves salesmen are really order-takers and in fact, are not even good order-takers. Some sales people barely make a living while there are some in the same profession who make a killing. How can a sales professional who sells identical products in the same market, for the same company, make 10, 20 or a 100 times more money than others?

While I was doing the demos of vacuum cleaners, where most sales people quit out of frustration because they couldn't make a sale, there was one employee who was one of the top salespersons in the country. He narrated an incident where on one day alone he made 24 sales, something many sales people don't do even in a few months. One day, there was a major snowstorm and there was close to 12 inches of snow. In Toronto, during the winter season there are a few days like this every year. Schools and offices are closed because

---

**Ability teaches us how to Do.
Motivation decides why we Do.
Attitude determines how well we Do.**

---

it becomes too risky to go out in such weather. Most sales people look at this as a great opportunity to stay at home and watch TV, but this person saw a great opportunity, for 2 reasons:

1. He realized that everyone would be at home that day. So, his chances of getting people through cold calls would be close to 100%.

2. Normally, vacuum cleaner demonstrations are in the evening or on weekends because if one person sees it they don't take a decision till they have consulted their spouse, and many times, it may just be an excuse, but chances of losing the sale become higher. But that day both decision-makers would be there. If the client is serious then it would save him a second trip to give another demonstration. Hence, he saves time.

He also realized that all his neighbors were prospects. They all had the same need. They were buying the same thing from somewhere else and he too was driving 10-30 miles away on appointments for demos. Why not sell in his own neighborhood?

He put on his snow shoes, clad himself well to walk in the snowstorm and carried his vacuum cleaner. He knocked on his neighbor's door and said *'Hello, I am John your neighbor. It's a shame that we haven't met earlier. We help families like yours live in a good healthy environment. Would you mind if I came in and shared some ideas with you or gave you a short demonstration?'*

9 out of 10 invited him in and since they were not doing much and were indoors anyway, they said go ahead. Then,

he did his full demo without being rushed and since both partners were there, decision-making was easy.

Just analyze the above scenario or approach:

1. He knocks on the door, he is outside and they are inside. A natural human tendency is that if there is a person standing outside your door, in a storm and especially if he is a neighbor, you ask him to come in. The entry was much easier and on favorable grounds.
2. His introduction was more of a neighbor than a salesman.
3. He said 'We *help families like yours stay in a good healthy environment'* – Who is not interested in living in a good healthy environment? If you analyze the words he said – he didn't say I am from XYZ Company selling vacuum cleaners.
4. He takes permission to come in and do the demo.
5. Now, he demonstrates to them, letting them touch and feel. He shows them the advantage of owning a vacuum cleaner by actually using it to pull out hidden dirt from their carpets, curtains, mattresses, etc. that could be injurious to their children.
6. He collects all the dirt in a bowl, hands the bowl to them and asks the question,
   'As a loving parent or spouse, I am sure you would want your family to live in a healthy environment, wouldn't you?' The most obvious answer was yes.
7. Then of course, he answers objections in case there are any.
8. He finally ends up closing the sale.

Persistent positive or negative thoughts act as a magnet to the outcome. Look at the above scenario – what an attitude, what an approach, what an opportunity!

Was this person focused? Did he have a specific goal in life? Was he wandering aimlessly? Something crucial to remember – so long as you have your eyes on the goal, you don't see obstacles. The moment you take your eyes off the goal, you start seeing obstacles.

A good sales professional is like a driver who steers his way to his destination, rather than a passenger who is at the mercy of the driver. Failures, on the other hand, are living through hell. Their spirits are dead. They stop making efforts and they wait for things to happen. They feel helpless.

The easiest way to overcome insecurity is to rise above mediocrity. Mediocrity has no power to move the soul. Mediocrity gives a mediocre living, a mediocre income and nothing beyond. Millions of people die in obscurity without any achievement in life. They are the ones who are half-hearted, who keep thinking, hoping and planning to do something but they never actually do anything. They are the ones that watch the world go by. They talk more and do less. They have only intentions and no action.

To the mediocre, life is about passing time, making it from birth to death safely. To them life is an existence not living. The mediocre take every day as one more day. Their biggest challenge is to find a way to get through the day.

> **So long as you have your eyes on the goal, you don't see obstacles. The moment you take your eyes off the goal, you start seeing obstacles.**

They do nothing to make their today better than yesterday. Self-improvement is not on their agenda.

Don't settle for mediocrity. If you set high standards, very soon you will build the reputation of being a good professional with commitment and credibility.

On closer analysis, one discovers that the top sales people do not have any advantages such as higher education or a powerful or charming personality. Neither does a person have to be aggressive in sales. What really separates a successful salesperson from a mediocre one are 3 important attributes:

Attitude – Mental toughness
Ambition – Burning desire with clarity of goals
Action – Translating dreams into realities or potential into profits.

Each person has a unique way of selling. Uniqueness basically means lack of duplicity and presence of originality. It is the adaptation and evolution of an idea that gives originality.

A good professional engraves a lasting impression on others regardless of the product he is selling. Winners have an unending desire to achieve their goals. Financial freedom is only one component of success, but a very important one.

Positive Mental Attitude

If you study the life of successful professionals who have achieved financial independence ethically, you will find they all have one thing in common – they are all positive thinkers and positive doers. There is a tremendous relationship between thinking and success or failure.

Good professionals feed their mind with positive thoughts on a daily basis to remain positive. When I sold life insurance, once my manager asked me a question, *'Do you know the difference between winners and losers?'* Then he said something very profound, *'Winners form the habit of doing things that losers don't like to do. What are the things losers don't like to do? Well, they are the same things winners don't like to do either, but they do them anyway.'* Then he gave me an example. He said, *'Losers don't like to work hard. Winners don't like to work hard either, but they work hard anyway. Losers don't like to get up in the morning, winners don't like to get up in the morning either, but they get up any way.'*

This is like an athlete who trains and practices every day. Does he like to practice every day or does he want to practice every day? The answer is no. But he does it any way. That's what makes him a champion.

Discipline

Discipline is doing what ought to be done, when it ought to be done, whether we like it or not. Life is like push and pull. Sometimes, we push ourselves and sometimes we have to pull ourselves. We need both, just like an automobile needs both the accelerator and the brake. One without the other will not work or will cause damage, just like an

> **Discipline is doing what ought to be done, when it ought to be done, whether we like it or not.**

army without discipline is guaranteed to fail. Discipline is really the spirit that strengthens an army and gives courage and strength even to a small group to face big challenges.

The least a good professional can do is to do his best. Doing your best may not always be good enough. It is important to do what it takes to succeed in life. That is why a good professional always believes in continuous improvement.

A common cold can be treated by medication, but a positive attitude has to be developed over a period of time.

5

FORMULA FOR SUCCESS

The profession of selling can be exciting and rewarding, both financially and emotionally, or it can be depressing and frustrating. A lot depends on a person's attitude and how he handles success and failure. When we make a sale we are on an emotional high. However, when we make no sales, we feel rejected and dejected. When a salesperson realizes that the profession is not only about making sales, but involves helping others and solving problems, he becomes a professional.

To succeed in the profession of selling, one needs to develop proven and repeatable methods of selling which can give positive results consistently. One must qualify and lead the potential customers through an effective selling process in order to result in a positive outcome. In fact, there are no exceptions to this process.

While sales people go into the profession looking for independence and freedom, most good sales professionals realize that success comes from the commitment and self-discipline for continuous improvement. Those who become top performers realize that they need intellectual, moral and ethical support, sometimes a pat on the back and occasionally a kick on the bottom too. Just like an athlete needs a coach, a good sales professional also needs a coach. *The role of a good coach is to turn a group of people into a committed team where each person is a star performer.*

The profession of selling is rooted in understanding the problem and providing the right solution through the act of empathizing and honest persuasion to result in a mutually profitable commercial transaction. The profession of selling is like playing chess. A good player pre-empts many moves of his opponents and plans his moves accordingly.

A good sales professional can be compared to an aircraft with an auto pilot. Let me share my experience to explain what I mean. Once, in the days when security concerns were low, I was traveling on an international flight with my then ten-year-old daughter. I took permission from the captain to show her the cockpit and how he was flying such a complicated machine. We went in and found the cockpit was full of little gadgets and gauges. I asked the captain how the aircraft stayed on track in spite of so many variables, such as bad weather. The captain explained, pointing out the compass and red lights, which used to blink on and off, that sometimes the aircraft goes off-course, but the moment this happens the auto-pilot brings it back on track. I thought to myself that the same thing is true in human life too! Don't we all go off-track some time in life and don't we all need the auto-pilot to bring us back on track? What is the auto-pilot that brings humans back on track?

1. Values
2. Attitude
3. Ambition
4. Clarity of goals and purpose

Burning Desire

Success does not just happen. It is the result of practicing the principles that lead to success.

A young man asked Socrates the secret to success, Socrates asked him to meet him at the riverside the next morning. They met. Socrates asked the young man to walk into the water and he did. Socrates suddenly ducked the kid underwater and held him there till the kid started turning blue. Then, Socrates pulled him out. The first thing the kid did was to take a deep breath. Socrates asked him, *'Son, when you were under water what did you want the most?'*

The young man said, *'Air.'*

Socrates said, *'Son, there is no secret to success. When you want success, as badly as you wanted air when you were in the water you will have it. Nobody will be able to stop you that day.'* This is called a burning desire. This is the difference between preferences and convictions in life; preferences are negotiable, convictions are not; and under pressure, preferences always become weak whereas convictions become stronger.

Success does not happen and a reward doesn't come without action. Just as you cannot reap without sowing, similarly, dividends do not come without investing. Sales do not happen by sitting back. They are the result of tremendous hard work, effort and conscious action.

Motivation

Motivation is like a fire. Unless we keep adding fuel, it dies out, and fuel to a good professional is feeding the mind with positive thoughts on a daily basis without which de-motivation creeps in. A true professional is driven because they consider themselves self-employed.

Some people stop working the moment they meet their quota or target because they only want to keep their job, they are not internally motivated. They produce only enough, so that their supervisor has no reason to fire them. They do only enough to get by with. They are really not motivated. If they were motivated, they would go beyond the call of duty. Is there anything known as 'beyond the call of duty?' or is it a misnomer? Going beyond the call of duty is actually the duty! In fact, how can duty stop when more can be done! If you've done your duty, how can there be anything left beyond?

> **Is there anything known as 'beyond the call of duty?' or is it a misnomer?**

Getting motivated is probably easier than staying motivated, especially, in the face of receiving rejection a lot of the time. Staying motivated is not easy and is the

> **If you've done your duty, how can there be anything left beyond?**

true test of a professional. Different people do different things for different reasons. Some people run fast to win a marathon race or a medal at the Olympics. Others may run even faster if a dog is chasing them on the street. Some are motivated by positive rewards; others are motivated to avoid negative consequences. Some people sleep out of relaxation, others sleep out of exhaustion.

As good sales professionals, our objective is to provide positive motivation to the prospect to purchase. Hence, not only should we show a benefit but also how we can prevent a loss, i.e. desire to succeed versus desire not to fail. Both pain and pleasure can be strongly motivating. Those who are insecure often buy things that they cannot even afford only to avoid the feeling of inferiority. Some buy expensive cars, jewels and paintings only for prestige reasons, whether they can afford it or not. They are satisfying a need of inadequate self-esteem. The needs convert into wants. The desire to avoid pain can be a very strong motivator. Just because an ineffective salesperson is not able to uncover a need or a problem, it does not mean that the problem does not exist or that the client does not have a need.

Motivation is really the spirit in the person. It is the fuel in the car that starts the engine. Most people don't take the time to find out what motivates them. They have no goals to strive for, nor any benchmarks of values and ethics. Both goals and ethical standards drive behavior. Values such as integrity, respect, responsibility are the foundation of belief and commitments that drive behavior. You can only give what you have in

> **Both goals and ethical standards drive behavior.**

life. If you do not practice integrity, respect and responsibility with yourself, how can you practice it with anyone else? If I cannot be honest to myself, how can I be honest to anyone else? If I don't practice self-respect, how can I respect anyone else? If I am not responsible for my behavior, who is?

Is Family Pride a Motivation?

I have seen athletes do exceptionally well on one particular day and when asked *'How did you perform so well? What was motivating you today?'* Many times the answer is, *'My family is watching me today.'* or *'My family is in the audience and they have great expectations of me and I cannot let them down'* or *'I must make them proud.'*

On the Lighter Side – a business was running into problems because of very low sales and the deep deficit was marked in red color on the sales chart. The manager called in a consultant and started showing the territory, all the red colored demarcations and the pins holding them up. With great hope, the manager asked the consultant what he should do. The consultant said, *'The first thing you do when the sales people walk in Monday morning, is take these pins off and stick it in their behinds. **A carrot and a stick always work better than only a carrot'**.*

There is No Substitute to Hard Work

Athletes practice for 15 years for 15 seconds of performance. Success has no hard-and-fast rules. It has only 'hard and hard' ones. In fact, some people go into the profession of selling

> **Success has no hard-and-fast rules. It has only 'hard and hard' ones.**

with a casual approach and treat it as a part-time job.

A candidate went to a sales manager in the company and said, '*I am looking for a job where I can work half day only.*'

The sales manager said, '*We have the job, you have to decide which half-day you want to work, the 12-hour-day or the 12-hour-night, and the full day is 24 hours.*'

Evaluate if you have achieved competence in selling. Competence is the **will and the skill** to create a positive outcome leading to a win-win for all parties. The burning desire to succeed is the will and the ability to persuade with integrity is the skill. There are many skillful people who are incompetent, because they lack the will. To a good salesman every sale is exciting; it gives a person an instant high of gratification.

A career in sales opens an opportunity which is unlimited. It can mean a frontline sales position or selling a high-ticket item, business to business.

Buyer Motivation

Many times a prospect is not aware of his needs. Hence, it is the responsibility of a good professional to bring it out. By bringing out the need, we can motivate the buyer to take action.

For example, I was once told by a salesperson that I could save a lot of money by installing roofing insulation in my house to prevent heat loss. This motivated me to buy the solution offered which was otherwise invisible to me at that time.

At the same time, just because you have a solution it does not mean that every potential prospect has a problem. When the need is identified, it must be recognized with equal intensity by both the buyer and seller in order to conclude the sale. Some people may not realize that they are sitting on a potential problem. Just because the problem does not manifest itself today, they feel sometimes, rather strongly, that there is nothing to be fixed.

Hence, no matter how good your price is or value for money, it is perceived a waste. Some needs are visible, sitting on the surface, whereas others are hidden and need to be uncovered. Cars need regular maintenance to address both what we can see as well as what we can't. We seek to avoid future problems. The salesperson can motivate the buyer to act in his own best interests.

Formula for Success

1. Be passionate about the profession of selling.
2. Believe in your product.
3. Believe in your company.
4. Believe in being a good professional by practicing integrity.
5. There is no substitute for hard work.
6. Practice persistence, don't quit.
7. Be a possibility thinker. Always look at possibilities and potential. Be optimistic.
8. Be knowledgeable about your product, service and industry.

9. Get on a continuous education program.
10. Evaluate your performance, daily, weekly, monthly and with each evaluation, note 3 positive things you are doing and 3 things you need to improve until the next evaluation. Reinforce the positive and replace the negative.
11. Wise people learn from their mistakes but wiser people learn from others mistakes.
12. Be enthusiastic – it shows belief in your product and in your profession.
13. Empathize with your prospect. Put yourself in the other person's shoes.
14. Become a high energy person. It shows you have a clear destination and the determination to achieve it. Avoid burnout.
15. Build self-esteem and display self-confidence.
16. Don't procrastinate. Learn and practice the phrase – 'Do it now'. Don't be an escapist.
17. Develop pride in performance. No matter what you do, do it with great pride.
18. Don't do anything half heartedly. Let your work speak for you. When your work speaks for you don't interrupt with words.
19. Stand by your principles of integrity. Your credibility determines your profitability in life. It is your goodwill more than money.
20. Do the right thing, the first time and every time.

I would also recommend that you associate with people of high moral character because positive people reinforce the positive.

George Washington said, '*Associate yourself with men of good quality, if you esteem your own reputation, it's better to be alone than in bad company.*'

The following statement has a lot of merit '*Where you will be 5 years from now will depend upon the kind of books you read and the kind of company you keep.*' How true. Where we are today also is the result of the books we read and the company we kept in the last 5 years.

'*The quality of a person's life is in direct proportion to their commitment to success, regardless of their chosen field of endeavor.*'

– Vince Lombardi

Public Relations (PR)

Your pride in the profession helps to succeed through public relations. PR means that, without commercial advertising, you announce to the world that you exist by providing a useful service to society and making an honorable living. The difference between PR and advertising is that in an advertisement, you promote yourself soliciting business whereas in PR, a third party recognizes you and your work and because of that, people want to deal with you – with or without your solicitation. We need to understand clearly that PR is not self-promotion. It is recognition. PR is a crucial part of gaining credibility and visibility.

As a good professional, you need to expand your circle of friends. The easiest and the fastest way is to volunteer your time in an organization that is constructively involved in community development. You will immediately develop a large circle of like-minded friends with mutual respect.

It builds goodwill, and shows concern for the community or society, provided your involvement is for a cause and not just a strategy for improving sales. Improvement in business happens as a result of mutual respect because like-minded people want to deal with other like-minded people. Commitment to a cause should be genuine and not have an ulterior motive.

The following are some good options to get involved in:

a) Rotary   b) Lions   c) Round Table
d) Junior Chamber   e) Scouts and Guides
f) Red Cross   g) Cancer Society
h) Chamber of Commerce

There are many other similar organizations and self-help groups.

One can get involved by volunteering your time, donating money, sponsoring an event, addressing meetings (give speeches, run seminars and workshops) or informing local media (i.e. TV, radio and newspapers) that you are available for discussion when they call guests.

Bragging is not PR

In order to establish credibility, some people think that blowing their own horn would help them overcome all the negative perceptions of the buyer. In fact many sales people start bragging about their personal and organization's achievements, as a strategy. Unfortunately, most of the time it backfires. People prefer a subdued, humble and soft approach rather than an approach to show how great they are. When a medical doctor approaches a patient for the first time, the first few seconds or minutes gives the patient a feeling of comfort or discomfort. At that point the doctor's people skills are more crucial than his professional skills. The patient doesn't care if the doctor came first in his class at medical school. It is both the people-skill and professional-skill that start developing credibility and confidence in the buyer.

Input Determines Output. Your success or failure is determined by the ratio of risk and trust between the buyer and the seller. The risk and the trust factor are in inverse proportion.

Recipe for Failure

Poor attitude + Poor values + Poor planning + Poor marketing + Poor selling + Poor service = Quickly out of business

Poor planning + Poor marketing + GREAT SELLING + Poor service = Frustration + burn out = Out of business

Great planning + Great marketing + GREAT SELLING + Poor service = Frustration + burn out = Out of business

All 3 scenarios above lead to:

High risk + no/low trust = Out of Business, Frustration and Burnout

Suspicion makes both parties to remain on the defensive. It's caused by a lack of transparency and also results in further loss of transparency. It becomes a vicious cycle and can eventually lead to a confrontational relationship. Always ensure to stay away from such situations as they lead to distrust and suspicion.

Recipe for Success – Will and Skill

Great attitude + Great values + Great planning + Great marketing + Great selling + Great services lead to **High Trust + No/Low Risk = Growth, Prosperity and Success**.

To sum up: Selling is like cooking a dish. In order to get a delicious dish, you have to have the right ingredients, right quality and the right proportions cooked at the right temperature and mixed in the right order. Similarly, if any one of these items is poor, it is a recipe for disaster. It doesn't matter what combination it is.

6

QUALITIES OF A WINNING PROFESSIONAL

Edison said that *'Success is 95% perspiration and 5% inspiration.'*

What are the qualities of a winning professional? They are what are called the 6 Cs:

Character	Makes ethics a way of life
Courage	Courage to continue despite setbacks
Conviction	Has belief in his product, profession and organization
Clarity	Has clear goals and purpose of life
Competence	Has the skills and the will to sell
Communication	Persuasion skills and ability to convince.

Selling is both an art and a science. Selling is an art because you are dealing with humans who are unpredictable. They are creatures of emotions, and emotions invariably override logic. It is also an art because it takes creativity to be a good sales professional involving innovation and uniqueness with each prospect. It is a science because by following a certain series of steps, in sequence, your closing ratios and probability of making the sale becomes much higher. It is also a science because it is based on certain principles which if repeated will produce the same or similar results. To take the mystery out of selling we need to convert selling from an art to a science. It means we need to follow certain processes and principles consistently in order to get consistent results.

A person does not become a professional doctor by just having the desire to be one. He must gain competence, education and training at a medical school to become proficient. Similarly, a good sales professional must learn the art of applying the principles of selling scientifically and with proficiency.

Essential qualities of a good sales professional:

1. Healthy self-esteem

A good professional lives by the motto, '**Customer first, commission second**'. They have pride in their performance, company, product and profession. With this pride, they go out to the customers from a position of strength. Their behavior and actions are not apologetic.

2. Good Communicator: Listening and persuasion skills

They are the ones who ask relevant questions and listen carefully to identify the needs of the client and provide the right solution. The unprofessional or the typical salesperson is the one who talks too much. In fact, he talks to the point of losing the sale. A good professional explores and uncovers a customer's need. He is there to assist and help, not to manipulate.

3. Belief and conviction

A good sales professional is sincere and excited about his product. Every morning, he gets up looking forward to providing solutions to his customers. He strongly feels that those who don't own his products or use his services are losing out or being deprived of something valuable.

4. Know your company or product

A president of a dog food manufacturing company was very disturbed because the sales had gone down badly. At the annual national conference, while he was addressing a few hundred sales people and becoming very emotional, he said, *'I don't understand why our sales are not picking up, even though we have some of the best packaging and some of the best graphic designing. We advertise heavily and have a large sales team too. I don't understand why we are not selling more dog food?'*

One person got up and said, *'Sir, did you ever ask the dogs if they like your food?'*

1. The more knowledgeable you are about your company and product, the less chance there is that you would over-promise and under-deliver.

2. You will be much more confident in making and keeping your commitment for price, delivery, etc.

3. You will be in a better position at handling problems, and troubleshooting in a more precise manner.

4. You will know the values of your company. Hence, your level of flexibility is clear. It brings clarity as to what you will stand for and what you will not stand for. You know the situations in which you will walk away from doing business.

A professional salesperson does the following:

1. Gains new customers
2. Retains existing customers
3. Generates new business from existing customers
4. Establishes a relationship of trust with customers
5. Becomes a permanent resource to his customers
6. Helps customers become more productive and profitable
7. Provides after-sales service
8. Builds credibility and goodwill with customers
9. Acts as a source of feedback and market information for his company.

Unprofessional Sales People	Average Sales Professional	Exceptional Sales Professional
Money driven	Company driven	Goodwill and customer driven
Selfish	Self-interest	Mutual interest
Doesn't do the right thing	Does the right thing for the wrong reason	Does the right thing for the right reason
Attributes success to luck	Takes full credit for success	Takes credit and gives credit to those behind the scenes
Does as little as he can get by with	Tries to only stay on right side of the law	Does work ethically
Big ego driven	Prestige driven	Performance driven
Wants to make money	Wants to make sales	Wants to make customers

Continuous education

Career-minded sales professionals go on a continuous improvement program in order to excel in their field. These are the top performers.

Experts feel that a person who invests just 5 to 7 hours a week in education can in 3 to 5 years become an expert in their chosen field. Continuous education helps broaden horizons. It makes a person knowledgeable in their product and helps understand people's psychology. In order to master selling one needs a lot of training.

Once, a wood cutter worked for a company for 5 years and never got a raise. The company hired a new person and within a year the new person got a raise. This caused resentment. The person who had been working there longer went to his supervisor and asked, *'How come the new person got a raise and I didn't in the last 6 years?'*

The supervisor said, *'We are a results-oriented company. His output went up so he got a raise, if your output goes up you will also get a raise.'* So the man went back and he started hitting harder and putting in more hours but his output still didn't go up. He thought to himself that maybe the new person knows something more than he does. He went and asked him *'How come your output went up?'*

The new man said, *'After cutting every tree I take a break for 2 minutes and sharpen my axe. When was the last time you sharpened your axe?'*

The wood cutter said *'Oh! Oh! 6 years ago!'*

This story explains it all. Continuous education is like sharpening your axe. Good professionals are always on a continuous education program in order to sharpen their axes.

A person who can read but does not read is no better than the person who cannot read anyway.

7

PLEASING PERSONALITY

To create a positive impact you need to have a pleasing personality. A pleasing personality is a composite of overall behavior, appearance, verbal and non-verbal communication, dressing, grooming, etiquettes, manners, etc. The composite personality reflects in our '**people skills**', which is the starting point of rapport-building.

You are an ambassador

A salesperson is an ambassador for both his product and the company. No matter where we go and what we do, we always represent something or someone; hence, we are always an ambassador. To the customer, the salesperson is the company. The customer forms an impression of the company by the behavior of the salesperson. A favorable or unfavorable impression created by the sales person determines the attitude of the purchaser towards the company. He starts evaluating the company, based on the salesperson's behavior. Our courteousness, politeness and integrity exemplify anything and/or anybody that we represent.

Everyone is a salesperson for their company or the country. A case in point – We have an office in Singapore. I gave a taxi driver a business card to take me to a particular address. When we arrived, the meter read $11. I pulled out $11 but he took only $10. I asked, *'Henry, your meter reads $11. How come you are only taking $10?'*

He replied, *'Sir, as a taxi driver I am supposed to take you straight to your destination. Since I didn't know the last spot, I had to circle around the building. Had I brought you straight here, the meter would have read $10.'*

What he said thereafter touched me the most. He said, *'Legally, I can claim $11, but ethically I am entitled only to $10.'* He then added, *'I am not a taxi driver; I am an ambassador of Singapore.'*

When a tourist comes into a country after clearing emigration and customs, the first person he usually meets is a taxi driver. If the first experience of the visitor with the taxi driver is unpleasant, the balance of the stay may not be very pleasant either. The tone is set from the outset quite often. What this taxi driver was saying in unsaid words was very profound. *'I am a diplomat of Singapore without a diplomatic passport.'* He demonstrated through his actions pride in himself, his profession and the nation. As far as I'm concerned, Henry could qualify to be a visiting faculty to give a lesson on ethics at any leading university in the world.

First impressions

Whenever I go for an important appointment or meeting, I prefer to go wearing my suit and tie. When I am flying to my destination, my luggage may not reach on time and hence, I always carry a suit, tie and a white shirt in my hand bag. I am really not a suit-and-tie person but my first meeting generally is in formal clothing. Why? This is **because we never get a second chance to create a first impression.**

First impressions are crucial because people start forming opinions about one another within the first 3 or 5 seconds of meeting, even before a person says anything. We form initial impressions of one another based on appearances or visuals. If a sales professional has not gained the attention of the prospect within the first 30 seconds, it will be difficult for him to gain it later.

The first impression we give to people could either be positive or negative. The prospect starts making judgments based on those impressions, and feels comfortable or uncomfortable accordingly. Therefore, a good professional should reflect:

1. Confidence without arrogance
2. Friendliness without being over-friendly
3. Expertise without the 'I know it all' attitude.

First impressions include body-language, gestures, posture, shaking hands, smile, eye contact, attire, manners, etiquette and greetings. Sometimes, a person is greeted with folded arms, a blank or confused look, a cold stare or fidgety hands. One must be cognizant of all these signs. Either they establish trust or they create distrust. Hence, in order to create winning first impressions, the following are important:

- Appear well groomed.
- Look neat and clean, not uncouth or shabby.
- Dress formally for business appointments, especially when you are going for the first time. Preferably, dress in a way that is one notch more formal than that of the potential client.
- Don't be over-dressed or too casual.
- Greet with a warm smile and a firm handshake. (Firm handshake does not mean crushing the other person's bones.) The handshake should show warmth and not be a test of strength.
- Wear pleasant-smelling cologne or perfume and not one that is overpowering.
- Mannerisms should be gentle, not edgy or jerky.
- Be observant of the surroundings.

The above points may help establish a rapport, but the opposite behavior can kill the deal in no time. A negative first impression could eventually lead to loss of a sale and eventually the business relationship. Many times, the door closes permanently. It is of utmost importance that our appearance and mannerisms be pleasant and courteous.

The Way We Dress

A sharp, clean, conservative look is like a fruit for all seasons. It is not an uncommon sight to see sales people dressed shabbily. Not brushing your teeth, dirty shirt collar, untidy hair, body odour, bad breath or sweat shows lack of pride and attention in appearance. A shabby appearance is a turn off and can be offensive to anyone, leave aside a potential customer. Why sabotage your own success?

There is a flip side to this as well. There are some people who are permanently over-dressed and wear flashy clothes and jewellery. They are moved by fads and ads.

Conservative clothes are always in fashion. Somehow, it gives a feeling of stability, balance and maturity. A poor appearance will be responsible for a certain percentage of loss of sales, no matter how good your presentation may be. A dignified appearance inspires confidence.

Manners and Courtesy

Positive and polite words always lead to pleasantness

Gentleness inspires confidence and makes a person attractive. There may be times when you meet people who are discourteous or rude, but it does not mean that you change your behavior as well.

Once, a man, out of courtesy, opened the door for a woman as she walked in. She was rather obnoxious and said, *'Women are equal to men; hence you don't need to hold the door for me just because I am a woman.'*

The man replied, *'I am not holding the door for you because you are a woman, I am holding the door because I am a gentleman.'*

Rapport-building

For a good impression, one has to build rapport, gain confidence and build trust with the prospect because the first sale is that of the salesperson himself. This is where social skills play a very important role and a pleasing personality becomes very essential. Basic courtesy and manners are all starting points. The presentation and uncovering the need comes later, which will only happen if the salesperson has sold himself first.

Establishing rapport means creating a positive impact or a favorable impression before you start your presentation. Don't ever underestimate the power of courtesy and proper etiquette. Rapport-building is not the same as socializing or getting into long unrelated conversations.

Some people think that the best way to establish rapport is to have a little social interaction and to try and find out some common areas of interest. I must say that common interests can certainly be helpful, but many a time, sales people get carried away and overdo the socializing bit to the point of inconveniencing or irritating the prospect. Be careful with your socializing. If your prospect wants to talk of something other than business, make sure you don't ignore him. Be courteous, answer and then ensure that you get back to your business discussion.

A more professional way would be to shake hands, look confident, be pleasant, courteous and business-like.

Rapport-building could mean a sincere compliment or a positive statement.

For example, if you appreciate the decor, a statement of this nature by the salesperson may be appropriate – *'I must say this office is very tastefully done.'* The most important thing here is sincerity. The key is to appreciate only if you are sincere. Don't make insincere statements as people can sense falsehood.

Rapport-building leads to a trusting relationship and a feeling of comfort, resulting in sales.

8

SELLING IS A REJECTION BUSINESS

The Law of Averages

Success is not measured by how high we go up in life, but how many times we bounce back after we fall down.

One should keep in mind that even the best salesperson in the world cannot sell to 100% of his prospects and the worst salesperson may possibly sell to one by default. A sale made by default is not called selling, it is called peddling.

In the selling profession, there are more rejections than approvals and acceptances. To the amateur salesperson, rejection becomes very stressful and he is unable to handle it. This is because he takes the rejection personally. It lowers his self-esteem resulting in de-motivation and inaction. He doesn't realize that possibly his product or company is being rejected or because the customer may not want to buy at that particular time. Just because a person has said no to buying your product today, he is not saying that he will never buy it in the future. It is nothing personal. An exception could be when a salesperson's discourteous behavior to a customer may lead to total rejection of the product.

> **Success is not measured by how high we go up in life, but how many times we bounce back after we fall down.**

When I started in the insurance industry, my manager taught me the law of averages. During my training he told me that I would have to make about 150 calls and will be able to speak to about 50 decision-makers, with the others being unavailable for some reason or the other. If I spoke to 50 people, I would end up with 12 appointments to see prospects face-to-face, to whom I would make presentations to sell life insurance. These appointments were always made 1 week in advance. If I had 12 appointments lined up, 2 might get cancelled at the last minute and I would end up making 10 presentations. If I made 10 presentations and if I was a bad salesperson, I might probably sell 1. If I was average, I would end up selling 2, but if I was good I might end up selling 3 or 4 and if I was excellent, I would sell 5 or 6. The objective of the good salesperson is to raise their average from good to excellent and that's what makes Michael Jordan or Sachin Tendulkar the superstars they are.

The law of averages can be explained by the risk-and-reward ratio. If the prospect feels the risk is greater than the reward (trust) in dealing with you, your chances of closing the sale go down. The reverse is just as true. If the rewards (trust) are greater than the risk for the prospect, your probability of closing the sale is higher. Our objective is really to reduce the risk factor and increase the reward factor, which will raise our closing ratio and improve our average.

Just as a prospect considers the risk-and-reward ratio, a salesperson also faces the risk of rejection every time he makes a call. If he focuses on the reward, his chances of remaining motivated are higher, because let's face it, every rejection does hurt our self-esteem. Rejection can be intimidating and shake the confidence of even a seasoned salesperson.

Fear of Failure

Negative emotions like fear, hate, jealousy and anger result in internal battles that drain us of our energy. Fear of failure is worse than failure itself. In fact, it drags a person to failure. Self-doubt gives one a feeling of depression and uncertainty. Whether the prospect will buy from me or not is a question that might be constantly nagging the mind of a salesperson. This increases the worry of whether one can sell the product to the customer or not. This becomes a chain reaction. Failure leads to more failures because with every failure, a person's self-esteem goes down and it becomes easy to fail the next time. Soon, this salesperson starts blaming the whole world for his failure. He blames his territory, bad prospects, bad manager, bad product, bad company, bad luck and bad everything, except himself. Negative people are driven and controlled by fear. The sad part is that most of the time the fear may be imaginary. Real fear ought to and can be addressed. Even imaginary fear can be addressed.

What is required is changing one's self-image. The moment a person does that, his life takes a different turn. Now, he starts understanding that in the same territory, with the same product and under the same circumstances there are some people who break records while others break themselves. Fear of failure leads to expectancy of failure. When people attempt with a negative expectancy, they start half-heartedly and end up failing. They then say *'Didn't I tell you, I wouldn't be able to do it and see, I couldn't do it.'* They prove themselves right. Failure becomes a self-fulfilling prophecy.

Low Self-esteem

Putting on a false mask and pretending to be someone that you are not is a sign of low self-esteem. Acting and looking important is useless unless a person feels that he is important, and feels he has something that will benefit the potential buyer. The feeling of importance is not a matter of false ego or putting on false airs. It is self-respect and dignity. It is pride in your work and poise in your behavior. Your behavior will be reflected in your closing ratio.

With the same product and under the same circumstances there are some people who break records while others break themselves.

Selfishness and jealousy are 2 major evils that result from low self-esteem and insecurity. Low self-esteem makes a person compromise on values. The more they compromise on values, the lower their self-esteem falls, which makes it easier for them to compromise on values again. This then goes on to become a cycle of little dishonesties and failures, leading to a final disaster.

The straight and sure-shot path to self-respect and confidence is having integrity and honesty. Honesty is displayed when a person is in the habit of telling the truth. Unfair and unjust dealings carry a price tag that eventually the dishonest person has to pay. A good principle to live by is honesty and fairness to yourself and others in all dealings. Honesty is a virtue, not a policy. It is a way of life. Virtues represent purity and integrity of thoughts and actions. Therefore, a person who lives with honesty and integrity will always have high self-esteem and can consequently make an excellent career in sales.

Loser's Profile
Why Sales People Fail? Is Success Really a Matter of Luck?

> 'Success is merely a matter of luck. Ask any failure.'
>
> – Anonymous

To amateurs, meeting targets and deadlines is stressful and de-motivating instead of motivating. They develop an escapist behavior and start negative habits like drinking and smoking, in order to get away from commitment. They look for artificial ways of relaxation. They try to practice high pressure and manipulative tactics to make a sale, which can backfire easily.

To some, the profession is like a war to be won; some look at the prospect as a scapegoat; and for some, getting rejected is very stressful to handle. Hence, with these attitudes, they burn out. Bad sales people are always on the verge of quitting the company or waiting to be asked to leave the company. The average and the good ones maintain their jobs and make a living, but the excellent ones make a career and a killing. The 80:20 principle applies pretty much across the board in most organizations – 80% of people produce 20% of the sales. Reverse is also true. 20% of people produce 80% of the sales.

Winners do things in spite of problems, and losers permanently rationalize in life and make excuses. They are the moaners, groaners and complainers. They always wait for things to happen, they never make things happen. They are the ones who come in the morning and say, *'I just came in, let me get settled.'* After half an hour of settling, they say, *'I need a cup of tea to wake up'* and then waste another hour chit-chatting, socializing, thinking they are building relationships. That brings them to around 11 am and one-fourth of the day is lost with zero output. At this point they say, *'Let me get to work and catch up now.'* Then they start searching for what to do and who to call. That takes them to 12.30 pm. They look at the watch and say, *'What is the point of calling at this time? It is lunch time and if we call, nobody will be there.'* They themselves will go for lunch. They will wait till 2 pm and then say to themselves that *'People must be busy with their work and who is going to talk to me.'*

They shuffle papers and keep disturbing others in the office. They need tea/coffee immediately after lunch to wake up. Finally, they make a few phone calls and as expected they get rejections. They rationalize by saying that *'nobody wants to talk to me'* or *'everyone is busy'*. At this point, they need another break to re-energize and they look at the watch. three-fourths of the day has gone by with no result. At the fag end of the day, they think of calling some more people, but they rationalize thinking that *'everybody must be planning to go home and so who would want to talk to me?'* This way the complete day is lost. They go home and complain that business was bad today.

Next day, they go back to office and repeat the same routine, demoralizing others, telling them that the company's product is not good, the company is not good, the boss is not good, the economy is not good, etc., and that, *'we must start looking for another job.'* This is the loser's profile. These people are getting ready to get ready but they never do.

Achievers and non-achievers are given the same time – 24 hours a day, same company, same product, same territory. Is it a wonder then that 20% of the people make 80% of the sales?

Great achievers, whether a scientist or an artist, did not waste time waiting for an inspiration. They kept working every day just like most good professionals, who routinely continue to do what is required of them.

Mental Toughness

All of us have good days and bad days. There are days when we get up in the morning, the world looks good, productivity goes up and relationships are a lot better and no matter what we do, everything comes easy. And then there are days when we get up in the morning and don't feel good. Our energy levels are low and we feel terrible. What happens on these days? Productivity goes down, we fight with everybody and no matter what we do, it takes a lot of effort to get even the simplest of tasks done.

The sign of a good professional is that whether it is a good day or a bad day, their output and performance is constant. On good days, it comes easy, but on bad days it takes a lot of effort. They, however, don't compromise on their quality and standards. This is called mental toughness.

Selling is a rejection business; you get more 'nos', than 'yeses'. To some, every rejection is dejection, but to a good salesperson it is an opportunity to bounce back and to turn severe setbacks into comebacks.

To them NO = Next Opportunity.

During my insurance selling days, I remember one of the top producers in the company. When he made calls for prospecting, to him every no was a time to celebrate. His attitude was I'm getting closer to my next 'yes'. And he used to qualify for the million-dollar round table.

A champion, whenever he is knocked and counted down, musters his internal strength to get up again. This is what makes him a winner. An athlete who trains every day, is learning through a process that takes self-discipline. Sometimes the training is fun and sometimes it's not, but the athlete trains nevertheless.

Self-image

Self-image is the way we see ourselves and self-esteem is the way we feel about ourselves. Our behavior depends on our conception of ourselves. Our success or failure in the external world will depend on this view in our internal world. If you believe yourself to be a person of character, courage and integrity, then all these traits will reflect in your behavior.

Many successful people have a positive personality which is reflected in their self-confidence and the aura around them. They have a sense of self-respect coupled with humility. Our self-conception and behavior is instrumental in the way others perceive us. In fact, everybody wants to associate and deal with successful people.

Our positive self-image makes us walk confidently and with energy, whereas a negative self-image makes us drag ourselves and our self-doubts are reflected in our behavior. Just like enthusiasm is contagious, so is lack of it. Your self-confidence gets transferred to the buyers and generates confidence in you, your product and company.

Confidence

A prospect also treats a sales professional who radiates confidence much differently than one who seems unsure and insecure. The prospect can feel the vibe of self-confidence and this makes him feel that he must listen to the salesperson as he may have something important to say. Have you ever wondered why some people pay more attention to some sales people and less to others? It is the sales professional's overall personality that makes all the difference. The salesperson's self-confidence makes the buyer feel that the seller has something important to say. What product you sell or company you represent becomes secondary.

The secretary who receives a business card from a confident sales professional takes the card to the boss and says, 'Mr ABC is here and it might be worthwhile to spend a few minutes with him.' If people feel that you are important, they will automatically show respect for you and your time.

An unimpressive salesperson might just be kept waiting at the reception, whereas a confident-looking person might be attended to immediately. A sales professional who radiates confidence is more likely to get uninterrupted and undivided attention whereas an unimpressive salesperson might be interrupted with many things that the prospect feels may be more important. The prospect may just be talking on the phone or reading the papers or clearing mail.

Persistence or Pest

Distinguish between being persistent and being a pest. **Persistence** is the ability to bounce back after every rejection. It is this ability that prevents a rejection from becoming a dejection. However, being a **pest** is when a salesperson becomes too pushy, starts nagging and irritating the prospect. He does not get the message that the buyer wants to be left alone. The 'pest' starts getting ignored. The prospect's patience is exhausted and chances of retaliation become higher. So, be persistent, not a pest.

Lack of persistence can cause you to lose the deal. You actually end up selling for your competitors and making them richer. Experience shows that 80% of the sales are made after the fifth call and that 80% of the people quit before the fifth call. This is called 'selling for your competitors'. The 80% who quit have now prepared the ground and made the buyers ready to purchase. They have done the difficult work, but when the time comes to close the sales, they run out of steam and they quit. Now, when the competitor calls and sees the client ready to purchase, they come and close the sale. You have actually made the sale for your competitors.

'You have damaged your own sale, by not being persistent.'

Perseverance does not mean that you bang your head against the wall. You will only end up with a head injury and the wall will still be there, as it is. We must understand the difference between will-power and won't-power. Will-power is persistence, won't-power is obstinacy. Whenever there is a tussle between water and a rock, eventually water wins. The water wears down the rock.

Everyone wants to win in life but very few people are willing to pay the price to prepare to win. Only those who care to do little things carefully and with pride are the ones who will do the bigger things carefully and with pride, because that becomes a habit. That is when a salesperson's career can sky-rocket.

'Winning is not a sometime thing; it's an all time thing.
You don't win once in a while, you don't do things right

*once in a while, you do them right all the time. Winning
is a habit. Unfortunately, so is losing.'*

— *Vince Lombardi*

Obstacles

There is a prayer, 'God, don't lighten my burden in life, just
give me stronger shoulders.' None of us can escape trials. For
someone who wants to accomplish something in life, every
day is the judgment day. Only the strong-hearted have the
courage to face their challenges head-on.

Recipe for Behavioral Change – how to get rid of negative habits and build positive ones

Winners focus their strength on winning. Losers focus their
strength only on what they can get by with.

Selling is an inner game. 80% of selling is the result of
self-esteem, self-image and mental conditioning, and only 20%
is selling skills. The way you think and feel about yourself gets
communicated to others. If you feel good about yourself, your
product and your company, it gets communicated non-verbally
to the other person. If you think and believe that you are a
person of integrity, that too gets communicated non-verbally.
This is the process of mental conditioning.

Mental Conditioning

Mental conditioning is done through a process of auto-
suggestion and visualization. It is a process used by some of

the top sportsmen and athletes in the world. Visualization is a process of forming a mental picture. Mental pictures trigger emotions and feelings.

It means that good pictures create good feelings, positive pictures create positive feelings. Pictures of success translate into success in life.

Replay an incident in your life when you felt good. What was the experience like? Didn't it create:

1. A positive attitude?
2. A desire to achieve more?
3. Motivation?
4. A renewed effort?

Watch your words – especially self-talk. Negative self-talk pulls one down and positive self-talk lifts a person's spirit.

Auto-suggestions are positive statements of the kind of person you want to be or the things you want to do. You can write these statements and read them daily, preferably twice a day. They will act as a constant reminder. Supposing I want to get rid of anger, my auto-suggestions would be as follows:

- I am relaxed   and not   I don't get angry
- I am cool, calm   and not   I am not stressed
  and collected   or tense

Auto-suggestions must be in the present and not in the future tense:

- I am relaxed   and not   I will be relaxed
- I am cool, calm   and not   I will be cool, calm
  and collected   and collected

Read them twice a day, once in the morning when you wake up and at night before going to bed. These 2 timings are important, because:

1. When you wake up in the morning, the body is rested, the mind is relaxed and the sub-conscious is receptive. You feed your mind with positive information or messages and it sets the tone for the entire day.

2. When you feed your mind with positive information as the last thing at night, it works sub-consciously throughout the night.

Visualization

If you want to see results, auto-suggestions must be accompanied with visualization. If you practice auto-suggestions mechanically without visualizing, you will not see results. Form a crystal clear mental picture of the kind of a person you want to be.

Practice for a minimum of 30 days. In fact, people who want to stay positive and motivated practice this throughout their lives.

What makes some people more effective than others?

There is an old saying – 'If you keep doing what you have always been doing, you will keep getting what you have always been getting.' Expecting different results is defined as insanity. If we expect different results then it stands to reason that we need to change the input because input determines output.

Positive auto-suggestions and visualizations are a process of internalizing positive behavior, which in turn condition us for success.

'It is a funny thing about life; if you refuse to accept anything but the best, you very often get it.'
— *Somerset Maugham*

9

TRANSACTIONAL VERSUS RELATIONSHIP SELLING

Transactional selling occurs when on a short-term, one-time transaction, the salesperson's focus is only on achieving that single sale, without any consideration for the future.

Relationship selling is what happens when we convert a customer into a client. It is really a process of forming a business partnership, where each partner not only transacts business but is interdependent with a common growth objective.

Sales can be:

- B2B (Business to business)
- B2C (Business to consumer)
- Direct or indirect selling

B2B may have a longer sales cycle than a B2C. Regardless of who your end customer is, long-term growth in the profession of selling can only be made after laying the foundation of a strong relationship.

The essence of relationship selling is the transition from being a seller to a supplier.

The Difference

If I buy a photocopier from you, I have made a transaction and am considered a customer. However, if I start buying all my office equipment from you, I have developed a relationship and have become a client. I have developed a relationship because of which I (the client) keep buying more and more. That's the difference between transactional and relationship selling. A salesperson's philosophy is reflected in his behavior and performance.

Some people become very social and make friends by entertaining with the sole objective of doing business with them. Once the usefulness goes, the friendship also goes. It is unfortunate because it is very shortsighted; it's also insincere. One should keep in mind that just because a person is a friend does not mean they are under an obligation to buy from you. In my career, I have acquired clients professionally and built friendships later, versus making friends with the intention of doing business. Sooner or later, people uncover the ulterior motive.

I heard the story of a very successful car salesman who had an old client come up to him in his showroom. John greeted him warmly and said, *'I haven't seen you in a long time. How have you been? Where have you been?'*

The client said, *'I have been in town. It's just that I didn't need to buy a new car so I didn't stop by.'*

John said, *'Well, I thought we were friends and you don't have to buy a car every time you come here. It is nice to see you once in a while.'*

Is it any coincidence that he was amongst the top sales people in his company?

Sincerity is the Foundation of Relationship Selling

Every sale, if handled properly, creates an opportunity for more and bigger sales in the future. Repeat orders are bigger because the buyer has developed a comfort level and feels secure. This happens only if you have performed well in the trial or first order. Trial orders are meant to test people. Relationship selling implies long-term commitment, common goals, mutual respect, ongoing trust and cooperation. Informal relationships, many a time, get converted into formal alliances also, helping joint-marketing and co-branding.

Establishing a relationship is a series of steps, by and large in sequence only. Jumping steps or changing the sequence could be counterproductive.

Relationship selling means the following:

1. People buy people first
2. Then they buy from the people
3. Then they buy from the company

Have you been to a restaurant which is well-known for its delicious food? You go in and find the service and the waiter rude and discourteous. No matter how good the food is, would you like to go back to the restaurant again? The answer is 'never'. If relationships are important, the question is what builds relationships and what destroys them? It is a development process. Unfortunately, there are some people who would like to see it happen instantly. That's like an MBA who wants to start as a CEO with all the perks. It's like the soldier who wants to start as a General. It is a good fantasy but it doesn't happen in real life. An athlete doesn't win the gold medal overnight. He goes through a rigorous training process. The same holds true with the profession of selling and building relationships. Whenever we want to bypass the process, the results can be disastrous. Risk of failure becomes high. Building a relationship is a process, not an event.

People must feel good with the people they want to buy from. Building and maintaining relationships boils down to basically 3 broad categories:

1. Behavior
2. Events
3. Activities or actions

People are uncomfortable opening up with someone they don't know or trust. When aggressive sales people use high pressure tactics, buyers become defensive. When sales people start asking questions without creating a rapport or without taking permission, the buyers withdraw themselves. The seller must create an

> **Building a relationship is a process, not an event.**

environment of comfort and trust to invite the buyer to open up or engage in a two-way transaction. As the comfort level of the prospect increases, the risk decreases. In other words, the seller cannot close a sale without going through the series of steps required for selling, establishing rapport and credibility, uncovering the need or providing solutions and then closing the sale. Credibility and trust go together to help a prospect open up. In fact, they are the starting point of any relationship. The reverse is just as true.

Mutual respect is the starting point for all relationships. Hence, avoid damage and in turn having to do damage control.

Transactional selling	Relationship Selling
Commission based	Integrity based
May have ulterior motives	Sincere
Tactics based	Principle based
Product based	People based
Price based	Value based
Feature based	Benefit based
Short-term	Long-term
Hard sell	Soft sell
Gain	Gain + retain

Relationship selling is partnering   **Long-Term**
Transactional selling may   **Short-Term**
be manipulative

Sometimes, sales people, out of immaturity, may just be short-sighted and not necessarily be manipulative or dishonest. They may end up only gaining but not retaining customers.

The true objective of a good sales professional is not just to make a sale but to create clients because it take less effort to retain a customer than to gain a new one.

How to Turn relationships into Strategic Partnerships

If a customer realizes or feels that your input is critical to their success, especially long-term success, your relationship can turn into a strategic partnership.

Further, if the buyer perceives you as a vendor not easily dispensable and who meets their terms, you are on the way to turning a strategic relationship into a strategic partnership.

Ask yourself, if you lost the customer, would it mean a big loss to your company and a big gain to your competitors? If the answer is 'yes' then this account is your strategic partner. This does not mean that others are not. A strategic partnership is one where both parties feel that each one is critical to the other one's long-term success, and they will work towards helping each other's growth.

It is not unusual to find that 20% of your customers represent 80% of your business, which means that the 20% can be considered as your strategic partners.

If any one of them feels that losing or replacing the other is of no significance then the strategic partnership does not exist. If there is no impact from losing the account, a strategic relationship does not exist.

Strategic accounts need specific resource commitment through the year. They need to be monitored on an ongoing basis of quality benchmarks.

Initially, when a new client comes on board, generally THEY are in control. But over a period of time, if you convert them into clients, YOU start gaining a certain degree of control with your client. For example, whenever you have a new product, you go into the buyers' office. You just put your product on the table and many a time it is not unusual for the client to ask, *'Is it good? . . . Will it work? . . . Go ahead and write the order.'* This is because the rapport and trust was already established.

Selling and Customer Service is a Philosophy

True assets are the relationships. A sales professional must learn and understand the concepts of:

+ Selling and buying decisions
+ Selling and buying patterns
+ Sales and purchase processes

Relationships are built on service, timeliness, courtesy and integrity. An efficient professional should give such good service that his customers actually feel guilty if they ever think of dealing with that salesperson's competitors. The quality of service and relationship should be so strong that they should not even think of entertaining a competitor. Let's face it, service is what we are getting paid for, aren't we? Quality service is not an obligation but a responsibility. It is what makes the buyer feel good and it is the experience of feeling good that keeps bringing him back to us. It is the feel-good factor.

The feel-good factor, unless backed by performance and substance, doesn't last too long. When performance is missing, the pleasantness becomes hypocritical and irritable because the foundation of trust transforms into suspicion.

When performance and pleasantness come together, they can achieve the following:

+ Establish reliability and dependability
+ Show accessibility and availability
+ Demonstrate care and concern
+ Become a helpful resource in his area of expertise
+ Pre-empt and prevent problems
+ Create stronger bonds and ties for future business assurance
+ Become aware of new sales opportunities and emerging customers' need
+ Keep competition from entering this account
+ Convert a transaction into a relationship
+ Establish a source of referrals
+ Establish emotional connections

Our objective is to gain and retain customers. To gain, we must convert transactions into relationships. Convert customer satisfaction into loyalty. Convert minimum standards into quality benchmarks, employee mentality into entrepreneur mentality, and change the thinking from working for money into working for organization. The advantages of trust and good customer service can be translated into profits and affect the bottom line by:

1. Higher sales
2. Goodwill

3. Less inventory
4. Reducing the cost of correction by doing the right thing, the very first time every time.

Relationship selling creates a collaborative and cooperative culture which is based on common goals, mutual respect, mutual trust, transparency, joint planning, proactive decision-making, problem solving, performance measurement and celebrating success jointly. This is called a 'stake holder partnership.'

Never Forget a Customer and Never let a Customer Forget You

Why is it important to keep our name in front of the customer?

- Because our priority and the customer's priorities are different
- Out of sight out of mind
- Our customers, unless reminded periodically, forget us faster than we think
- Whenever the need arises since your name is right in front of the client, you are the most likely person to be called

Don't Take your Customer for Granted. Always Keep in Mind that He is being Solicited by Your Competitors

The time to build a relationship is when you are not looking for an immediate gain. The contacts should not be a solicitation of business or asking for referrals. Always be in touch. Find a reason to remain in touch. A good sales professional should have 6 contacts per year with each client. How do you stay in contact 6 times in a year? Here are some suggestions that have worked well for me and may help differentiate you from others:

1. Send a thank you letter immediately after sale. (A sample has been given below – It is the letter I used to send.)
2. Birthday and anniversary greetings.
3. Independence Day card or a Thanksgiving card. An Independence Day card shows your concern, beyond yourself as a human being. People respect those who take a stand for a larger cause, selflessly. Thanksgiving is another opportunity for expressing your gratitude to your customers, friends or close ones. People feel appreciated, they feel good. It builds their self-esteem. When they feel good by your actions, they want to be close to you. It motivates them to come back to you.
4. Similar occasions, relevant to the local culture.
5. Sending season's greetings or New Year cards are also good occasions to remain in touch. Greeting cards are nice but it has become so ritualistic. People get them by the dozens and yours may be one more card lost in the pile. Hence, many times I prefer to stay away from it.
6. Newsletters, may be twice a year. These can include news about your company, new products or next program. These could be solicitations in new business or a settled account. Keeping clients informed and updated about any new development in the industry.
7. A corporate gift or memento that can be displayed on the table or the wall or is in daily use and keeps your

name in front of the client, because clients need constant reminders. Caution: A corporate gift ought to be only a memento and not a bribe. A pen worth $10 is a memento whereas a pen worth $1000 is a bribe.

8. Sending clients articles of interest from newspapers or magazines.

Plus any others that you feel will be appropriate.

During my days of selling life insurance, I invariably sent thank you letters to my clients who made a new or repeat purchase. This is how my letter was worded:

Dear X,

I thank you for the courtesy extended during my recent visit. I appreciate the confidence you have placed in me by accepting my recommendations. I am sure the future will prove the wisdom of your decision. I look forward to working with you closely.

Regards,
Shiv Khera

That's it! Short and sweet.

I find that birthday and anniversary cards work better than seasonal or New Year greeting cards. The reason is that it is something very personal. You touch the recipients' emotions. You connect. The recipient feels good. It is again the experience of feeling good that connects people emotionally. The more personalized the interaction, the better the emotional bond. Look back in your life and see how many people, other than your immediate family members wished you on your birthday or anniversary. Probably very few. You might be able to count them on your finger tips. But the few who did, you do remember them, don't you? By sending a birthday or anniversary card, you automatically become part of a close circle which is like a family. As a note of caution, don't overdo it and get too personal as it could backfire. Maintain an appropriate distance and a degree of formality.

Be innovative and creative; that is what makes selling an art.

Consultative Approach

Become a resource to your buyers and suppliers. Become a troubleshooter. Whenever a customer thinks of your product, your relationship should have been such that they should immediately pick up the phone and call you. That's the level of comfort and confidence they should have in you. This kind of relationship builds goodwill and is highly appreciated by potential customers.

A good salesperson is like a doctor or a lawyer. A doctor examines, diagnoses and prescribes; likewise, a good professional becomes a permanent resource in his field.

He is perceived as an expert. Whenever a client has a medical or a legal query, concern or clarification, he picks up his phone and calls his lawyer or doctor. Similarly, your clients should call you for any questions in your field.

The Lifetime Value of a Customer

My experience in the life insurance industry is that over a period of time, a client buys many life insurance policies

(10 – 15 policies directly not counting referrals) for himself and his family as their needs keep changing. On an average, a person buys 6 to 10 cars during his lifetime. Repeat business is a windfall which is your true earnings. A good stockbroker, insurance agent or a car salesperson will confirm and ratify. It is relationship-selling that makes work easier and more lucrative as time goes by.

Besides repeat business, a major benefit of relationship-selling is that it leads to referrals which are the best source of prospecting. Referrals can be a two-way street – good professionals both get and give referrals. There is no better advertisement than word of mouth from existing clients.

I have been dealing with my real estate agent for the last 20 years. In fact, in most of the transactions I have not even been a part of the negotiation. This raises 2 questions – why have I not changed my broker and have other brokers not approached me? Of course, I have been approached, but I have chosen to continue doing business with my present broker. I have maintained my loyalty. Relationship-selling is powerful because business growth starts happening automatically.

When you first start in the profession of selling, you seek business and build relationships thereafter. But when relationships get built, then business starts seeking the good professionals.

Zero Defect

Henry, my taxi driver in our Singapore office, has been with me for the last ten years. The first day when I sat in his taxi, there was a newspaper lying on the seat. I picked it up and started reading. He asked me, *'Sir, do you enjoy reading the newspaper every day?'*

I said, *'Yes.'*

Then he asked me, *'Would you like me to pick the newspaper for you on a daily basis?'*

I said, *'Yes and I will be happy to pay for it.'* In the last ten years I cannot remember a single day when I sat in his taxi and he did not give me the newspaper, without my ever asking or reminding. I'm sure, in the last 10 years there must have been days when he went through crisis situations, but regardless of those, he delivered. Can you imagine 10 years without exception, giving 100% performance!

What did he demonstrate? A caring attitude, responsibility, commitment and pride in performance. This is called **'zero defect'**. Henry converted me from a customer into a lifetime client.

10

PSYCHOLOGY OF SELLING

Personality Classification

A lot of research has been done on personality types and they have been classified under various labels by different organizations and researchers. However, in my 35 years of experience in selling I have never made a conscious effort to analyze the buyer's personality, and nor have I tried to match my personality style to suit that person. In fact, I sometimes wonder how a salesperson can change their personality style from buyer to buyer. To me it feels a little contrived, though I believe in personalizing and being aware of the surroundings and circumstances in order to establish rapport.

Prospects Vary in Behavior:

Some are polite and courteous.	Others are rude and ill-mannered.
Some are very open and direct.	Others are not so open and beat around the bush.
Some take time deciding.	Others are reserved and take their decisions quickly.
Some are willing to take risks.	Others are very conservative.
Some are willing to listen.	Others only talk.
Some are calm and introverts.	Others are aggressive and extroverts.
Some are actively involved.	Others are laid back and passive.

Most people are a combination of a lot of these things. Some people are visually motivated – they like to see and look. Some are auditory motivated – they like to hear and listen. Some are physically or kinesthetically motivated, which means they like to touch and feel.

Good communication includes being sensitive to all of the above behaviors, besides knowing how to question, listen carefully, give feedback, observe and identify feelings.

Have I always been able to judge people's personality and behavior correctly? The answer is no. Can I change my behavior to suit every personality? The answer is no. Have I handled every situation satisfactorily? The answer is no. However, I feel that there are certain universal principles of appropriate and inappropriate words, behavior and actions. If applied correctly, they can bring positive results. In my experience, regardless of the personality styles, most people fall into 2 categories – **thinkers and feelers**. The thinker's decisions are guided by analysis and logic, whereas a feeler's decisions are guided a little more by emotions. Both are present in each individual and eventually they both must be satisfied as the saying goes, **'Logic opens the mind but emotions open the cheque book!'**

Emotional Appeal

Many a time during my own sales trainings, I heard my manager use words that literally painted a picture of a man who felt it was his responsibility to be considerate enough to provide for his family, in case, unfortunately, he wasn't there. He used to say, *'God forbid, if something happens to you untimely, who will take care of the food, clothing and shelter for John and Mary?'* This kind of question compels the person to think because it paints a picture that is both emotionally painful and appeals to their nurturing instinct.

A good professional understands the buying motive. Would buying life insurance appeal to a person's saving instinct or love for his family? Is a person buying a car as a status symbol or as a necessity? A salesperson in a shop selling clothes should be sensitive to a buyer's need as to whether the buyer is looking for designer labels or utility garments.

Good professionals use stories and analogies to reinforce the sale and make their point. This provides emotional security. For example: 'Our guarantee is as good as 24 carat gold.' Another example is: 'We are the McDonald's of our industry,' or 'We are like the Rolls Royce of this industry.'

I have also seen sales people use a combined analogy: 'Our product is like the Rolls Royce, yet we are a household name like McDonald's.'

Psychology of Asking Questions

A good sales professional would like to qualify his prospect by asking questions. Asking questions and listening carefully helps identify the psychological needs of the prospect.

Questions put you in the driver's seat and help you direct the presentation. By asking questions that give a prospect alternate choices, you don't give the buyer a choice between buying and not buying, but rather a choice between buying this or that. When a question is asked, giving choices to buy one or the other, if there is any inclination to buy, then psychologically, the prospect starts thinking which one to buy rather than to buy or not.

Psychology of a Buyer

There was a little girl who used to buy a pound of chocolates every day from one shop. One day, her mother told her to buy chocolates from another shop. The girl said, *'No mom, I want to buy from the same shop, because I get more chocolates from this shop.'*

The mother couldn't understand her daughter's answer because to her, a pound meant a pound. So, she asked, *'How do you know that this salesperson gives you more chocolates?'*

The little girl explained that every time he put chocolates in the packet, he would always add more after weighing. She always thought that the shop owner was giving her extra. The other salesman always put more chocolates initially and after weighing a pound took out a few. The little girl got the impression that the first salesman was giving more and the other one was taking away.

The little girl was getting the same amount of chocolates from both sellers, but psychologically and emotionally, she felt she was getting more from the one who was actually putting in less first and then adding more to make it a pound.

Difference between Price and Cost

Price is the initial outflow at the time of purchase whereas cost is over the lifetime of the product or the total outlay which includes, servicing, break down, repairs, etc.

People buy value for money, not price.

Whenever a sale is made, people buy the package and not the price. There is a big difference between cost and price. Something may have a low price but may cost more while others may have a high price but may actually cost less. Price is a one time, initial going in, outflow whereas cost is the overall outflow during the lifetime of the product.

A good sales professional is sensitive to his buyer's needs.

Psychology of Getting Commitment and Closing a Sale

Supposing someone asks a salesperson, *'Can you have this machine delivered Friday morning?'*

The salesperson replies, *'Yes, I can get it delivered.'*

The customer says, *'OK, thanks for the information,'* and goes away. What happened? Just analyze the interaction here. Why did the customer ask if the machine could be delivered by Friday? Obviously, he had an interest for having the machine delivered by Friday? Since the salesperson answered in the affirmative, the customer went away with only the information. Did the salesman get any commitment? Is he a sales professional? His company is spending thousands of dollars in advertising to attract customers and by not having adequate selling skills, he and his company both lost an opportunity to close a sale. This is throwing money out of your pocket.

What would a good sales professional have done in the same situation when asked, *'Can you have this machine delivered Friday morning?'*

A good professional would have replied asking, *'Would you like to have the machine delivered on Friday morning?'*

If the prospect says 'yes' he has bought the product and is committed.

If a prospect asks, *'Can I make a monthly payment?'*

An unskilled salesperson says, *'Yes, of course.'* The customer goes away thanking the salesperson for the information.

A good professional would reply, *'Would you like to take care of your investment on a monthly basis?'* If the answer is 'yes', the prospect has bought the product and is committed. This is the time to start writing the order.

Psychology – The 'Minor Decision' Close

Always help your prospect to make minor decisions which imply the purchase; it is then that the major decision comes automatically.

For example: a car salesman says to the prospect, *'It is obvious you love the car. The only decision you have to make is whether you would like to have manual or automatic transmission?'* By giving the decision regarding which transmission the prospect is actually taking, his decision to purchase the car has been made.

A salesman for a clothing line says, *'This dress looks beautiful on you. The only decision you have to make is whether you want it in pink or blue.'* The moment the prospect gives the decision on color, the prospect has bought the product.

The greatest presentation is wasted if the salesperson does not know when and how to close: **The timing and the technique of closing a sale, both, are very important**. A good professional has to know when the buyer is ready to buy and how to emotionally (psychologically) engage the buyer in the decision-making process.

At what point does a presentation result into a sale is hard to tell, but a sales professional with experience develops an instinct that makes him sensitive to recognizing that moment. It enables him to gauge the customer, as to how close he is with the buyer.

Never Give the Price Without Establishing the Perceived Value

When should a person give the price? A price should only be given after the sales professional has created a picture of a solution or benefit or created a perceived value. Sometimes, the prospect might interrupt and ask, *'Just tell me the price, what does it cost?'*

A good salesperson would answer, *'I would be glad to share with you the investment once I am able to evaluate what solution would be appropriate in your situation.'*

Sometimes, the buyer will abruptly or impatiently ask for the price, even before you start your presentation. In a situation like this, what should a salesperson do? There are many sales people who start throwing numbers and pricing of various products or services. To this the prospect may say, *'Thank you very much. I'll get back to you.'*

What is the biggest mistake the salesperson made? He gave away the price without establishing the perceived value. A good professional will never give the price till he establishes the need, the solution and the value of the solution because people buy the package and not the price.

A good professional would say, *'I'll be happy to quote the investment, provided we both agree that we have the appropriate solution that meets your needs. What if we are not able to take care of your needs?'*

Giving out the price without giving the benefit first will send a wrong message. It is misleading and meaningless and may hurt the salesperson. Inadequate information brings rejections.

> **A cardinal rule for a good sales professional – never give the price without establishing the perceived value.**

A cardinal rule for a good sales professional – never give the price without establishing the perceived value.

11

WHAT BUYERS NEED AND WANT

Buyers keep our business running. They are the reason for our existence. They pay our expenses and they represent our income flow. They allow us to be in business. It is crucial that we understand our buyers' needs because unless we understand them, we cannot meet them.

Are buyers not looking for reliable, competent and quality vendors? Of course they are. Buyers are willing to reward sellers who meet the following criteria:

1. **Positive attitude** – People with a positive attitude are attractive like a magnet, because they show their willingness and desire to serve. They radiate positive energy around them. Negative people repel other people.

2. **Empathy** – Helps put people at ease; it shows a caring attitude. Putting yourself in the other person's shoes

ensures that you would do the right thing and not take advantage of the other person's situation. It follows the golden rule: 'Treat others the way you want to be treated.' **For people with integrity, practicing the golden rule is not strategy but a way of life.**

3. **Reliability** – Shows that you keep your word and meet your commitments.

4. **Dependability** – It is the warranty or guarantee that you can be trusted.

5. **Credibility** – Trustworthiness of the salesperson and the organization. Build your identity and create your brand equity. Be labeled as trustworthy. Good labels help build brand equity. The opposite is also true.

6. **Enthusiasm** – It is infectious. A smiling attitude and willingness to go that extra mile to complete the task undertaken will result in customer satisfaction.

7. **Knowledgeable/Quality Product** – The salesperson can be a counselor and a guide as the customer relies on the expertise and knowledge of the salesperson. Educate the buyer. Give enough information to allow the buyer to make an informed decision. Display your competence.

8. **Timely Delivery/Speed of Delivery** – This refers to the speed of returning phone calls or the speed of responding to enquiries or breakdowns. Speed can become a major competitive advantage. What are your benchmarks – 2 hours, 2 days, 2 weeks, 2 years or never?

9. **Personalized Service** – A customer is a human being and not a number. Customers require individualized service because they are not just statistics or data at your

company. They are people with feelings and emotions and hence need to be treated with respect.

10. **A Winning Principle** – This is the principle of always under-promising and over-delivering. Unexpected pleasant surprises go beyond customer satisfaction. They lead to customer delight, which in turn creates a 'wow', resulting in customer loyalty. This keeps bringing the customers back to experience that 'wow' feeling again. When they have that feeling, they become enthusiastic and tell others about their experience. Hence, the word-of-mouth advertising and referrals lead to more business. This is called positive publicity.

11. **Professionalism** – Professionalism is a composite of all of the above. It means being friendly without being over-friendly, not taking the client for granted, not ignoring basic etiquette, not starting to take liberties and always maintaining decency. Use positive words. Avoid sarcasm, and controversial topics such as racism, religion or politics. Always remember that you are there for business and not to score a point. The moment a person walks into your showroom/office they have earned the right to courtesy, whether they buy anything or not.

12. **Sincerity** – Sincerity and genuineness with integrity is a winning combination. Make it easy for the customer to build his trust in you.

13. **Good Communicator/Listener** – Be a good communicator, especially a good listener. Use language that is easy to understand. Communicate to express, not to impress.

14. **Persistence** – Be persistent but don't become a pest.

15. **Respect and Recognition** – Treat the customer well. Make him feel secure, in control and important. By paying attention to a person's emotional needs, you'll be addressing the basic needs of a human being and you'll pull the customer towards you.

16. **Transparency** – Be open with your customer and don't make him feel that you are either hiding important elements in fine print or that you won't deliver what you promised.

17. **Responsiveness/Response time** – Responsiveness is an attitude, whereas response time is a quality benchmark.

Beyond great salesmanship and professionalism, the buyer, of course, is looking for an excellent product. Back up what you do with a high quality, dependable product and you have the formula of a winning combination.

In fact, in my experience, you may even be able to beat the competition that might have a slightly better product if your service levels are higher. The buyer is often prepared to pay more for superior service as well. You support your company's success by making service an integral part of the whole customer offering.

What are the things that buyers dislike?

1. **Dishonesty** – Dishonesty includes lying, non-disclosure or hiding of material facts, giving incomplete information or making exaggerated claims. All of these amount to

dishonesty because if the truth was known to the buyer, his decision may have been different. In these situations if a sale is made, it is dishonest.

2. **Shabby Appearance** – Lack of proper grooming, uncouth behavior, etc.

3. **Oversized Egos** – Braggers, people with massive egos, arrogant attitude and show-offs will turn the prospect away.

4. **Sweet Talkers, Smooth Talkers or Fast Talkers – To begin with, the foundation of these people is insincere and dishonest. These are those** people who are more interested in talking rather than in listening. They are the ones who come up with solutions even without knowing the problem. They give too much of information and confuse the buyer. They use slangs, jargons, abbreviations and verbiage that confuse people. Good professionals communicate in a simple and easily understandable language.

5. **Being Pushy** – Using high-pressure tactics to sell.

6. **Pests** – People who nag become pests and harass the prospects.

7. **Lack of Transparency; Unpleasant Surprises – Unpleasant surprises turn-off the customer; pleasant surprises keep the customer happy**. Customers hate unpleasant surprises because they feel cheated. Why? When they feel transparency is missing they start questioning the integrity of the salesperson.

Selling goes beyond salesmanship. Of course, the buyer is looking for a quality product and dependable service.

Whenever we think of competition, what is the first thing which comes to mind? 'Let's see what the competitors are doing? Let's check what the prices are, and then undercut.' If price was the only factor that drove sales, we would never need any salesperson.

According to an informal research, people are willing to pay up to 10–15% price differential, without a second thought, for 3 words – **quality, reliability,** and **dependability**. The higher the price tag, the more willing they are to pay the differential.

For example, if I buy an item for $10, what is 10% of $10? It is $1. If you cheat me for $10 I am not going to go bankrupt as I can easily sustain the loss. However, if I buy an item for $10 million, I would rather pay $1 million extra to protect my $10 million than save a million and risk the entire amount.

I have a client who bids tenders all over the world and their tenders run into several million dollars. Once the CEO said, *'Our bid price is invariably approximately 20% higher than our nearest bidder and we pick up the contract or business.'* Why? It's because of 3 words – **quality, reliability** and **dependability and they offer that**. Not only is it true in products and services but also salaries for employees.

Sometimes, people ask, *'What is the difference between reliability and dependability?'* Reliability refers to products and dependability refers to people, which means products are reliable and people are dependable.

Whenever a customer goes dissatisfied, ask yourself which need was left unfulfilled. Evaluate your own performance to learn from the last transaction. Make your next transaction better than the last one.

A recipe for failure is to start giving solutions without finding out the problems. Find out the priorities of your customer because each one is unique. This is what helps you to customize and adapt your presentation to suit their need. A sales professional who recognizes the special need of a customer and appeals to their buying motive, ends up selling more.

Meet the needs of the customer, in the following manner:

1. Realize that each customer is a major stakeholder in your company and without his support there would be no income. To make the customer feel more important, each one should be treated with courtesy and respect.
2. Understand that in serving a buyer we are not doing him any favor; we are only doing what we are supposed to do.
3. Be aware that our job is to find out the buyers' needs and wants and ensure that we fulfill them.
4. Know that each buyer wants to feel important; hence, he expects and deserves individual attention.
5. Buyers want to be able to trust their suppliers. Be cognizant of the fact that it's the trust which breeds loyalty.

It costs 6 to 10 times more to gain a new customer than to retain an existing one.

12

QUALITY AND CREDIBILITY

If you want to provide quality and you value your credibility, then live by this philosophy – **Always under-promise and over-deliver**.

Your ability to grow and prosper in a competitive world is going to be determined by how you get repeat business and how you bring new business through the door. The salesperson on the front line, is the person that interfaces with the customer and as the ambassador of your company, he is the one who will play the biggest part in how you are perceived by the outside world. The key aspects of building credibility are addressed below:

Knowledge

The salesperson should have an excellent knowledge of

the product, the company and of how to execute a sale professionally. As he walks into a prospect's office, he should know:

1) What are the 3 major strengths of the company and the product range?
   a) In absolute terms as well as in comparison to the competition.
2) How does the product work? What does it do?
3) What is your company's business history and philosophy?
4) What are your company's policies regarding:
   a) Guarantees and warranties
   b) Pricing, including negotiation
   c) Minimum quality standards
   d) Delivery and turn-around time
   e) Reliability and servicing.

Attitude towards Commitment

Before you make a set of commitments to a buyer, evaluate whether these are realistic and can be met with a high degree of surety. It is unethical to promise something just to secure a sale without even knowing if it is possible. Have you added a small safety-margin in case of possible delay? What would happen to your credibility and to that of the company when your commitments are not kept?

My family recently purchased some lights for our verandah. With a straight face, the seller promised that the lights would arrive ahead of the holiday weekend. We were reassured that regardless of the busy season, the merchandise would be delivered in a timely manner. Based on that we paid a deposit. The weekend came and went. The next weekend came and went and so did the one after. The lights were eventually delivered a month later and in the wrong color! It took another 3 weeks to get the right lights delivered. Where is the credibility of the seller? He not only failed in his commitments, but was also unprofessional enough to not care if he was delivering the right product or not. I will never buy from this person again and if asked by others, I will warn them of the potential poor performance.

I contrast this experience with one where I bought a new shower stall. The vendor was recommended by a family member. He showed up, gave me a presentation and a quote which was more expensive than another offer that I had, but I liked the way he presented me with the product options and I went ahead. Something gave me a good feeling. Every single promise he made was kept and the product was delivered before the due date. I was also very pleased with the stall when it was fixed. I paid him on the spot and I recommended him to 2 other people within the following week. It was a pleasure to work with him.

Attitude Towards Customer Service

In order to create a level of comfort in clients, it is important to focus on the level of service provided. When the client asks a question, what happens to the client's confidence in you and your organization? Does he feel secure or does it raise doubts in your ability to deliver. It is important to evaluate if you have established your benchmarks and quality standards. **Every little thing matters. If it matters, is it really little?** What a philosophy to live by!

Evaluate:

1) How quickly do you answer the phone?
   a) Is it a pleasant experience getting through to the right people?
2) How quickly do you return phone calls?
3) What is your response time for service and maintenance?
4) What is your response time in case of a breakdown?
5) How often are you in touch with your customers?
6) How often do you seek customer feedback to assess satisfaction?

Most customers, even if they had a problem with you or your product/company, would stay with you, provided they feel that you have a caring attitude and that you made efforts to resolve their problems. However, good sales professionals are proactive and prevent problems from arising. They constantly evaluate their relationship with the customer, checking the following indicators of dissatisfaction:

1) Indifferent attitude – customer is cold.
2) Customer keeps appreciating your competitors.
3) Increased number of complaints.
4) Buying volumes going down.

Every little thing matters. If it matters, is it really little?

A customer wants to feel that he took the right decision by giving you his business.

Who defines quality?   –   Always the buyer.
How do you build credibility?   –   Only commit what you can deliver.

Excellence and quality are the result of continuous training and testing. It's an on-going process. Good organizations need to train their staff on quality standards.

Striving for excellence is a sign of quality. Striving for perfection is neurotic. Is there anything known as perfection? Is there anything that cannot be improved upon or not be done better the next time? **Good professionals set high standards for themselves. They raise the bar to achieve new heights. They break their own records continuously.**

13

SELLING PROCESS

SELLING HAS CHANGED

FROM			TO		
Attention	–	10%	Rapport	–	40%
Interest	–	20%	Need	–	30%
Desire	–	30%	Solution	–	20%
Action	–	40%	Close	–	10%

How the Sales Process has Reversed

THEN

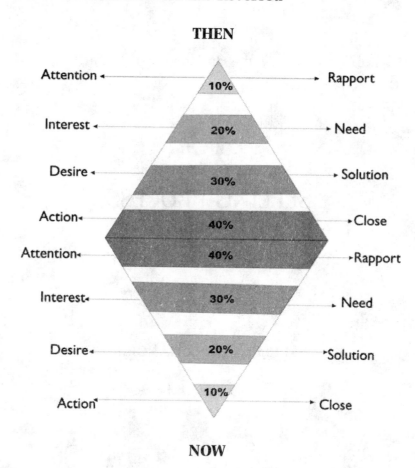

Attention ←	10%	→ Rapport
Interest ←	20%	→ Need
Desire ←	30%	→ Solution
Action ←	40%	→ Close
Attention ←	40%	→ Rapport
Interest ←	30%	→ Need
Desire ←	20%	→ Solution
Action ←	10%	→ Close

NOW

Steps in the Sales Process:

1. Planning
2. Preparation
3. Prospecting
4. Approach – Telephone or Personal
5. Attention

6. Establishing rapport
7. Presentation
8. Fact-finding
9. Uncovering the need – Questioning techniques
10. Creating a want
11. Presenting a solution
12. Trial close
13. Handling objections, if any
14. Reconfirm the answering of the objection
15. Trial close
16. Closing the sale by signing the order
17. Reinforcing the sale
18. Getting referrals
19. Keeping all your commitments which made the sale
20. Relationship-building to build loyalty

There is a saying — 'When opportunity meets preparation it is called "good luck"'

Does a good athlete compete without preparation? Does a captain manage his ship without preparation? Only professionals understand the value of preparing for a sale, and that's what drives their ability to capture the sales that slip away from those who have only prepared for one eventuality or who have not placed themselves in the mind of the buyer.

Once, I hired a new salesperson. He was going through the training process and role play. As he opened the presentation after introduction, he said to the prospective client, *'Well, I forgot to bring my laptop but I brought the CD. If you have a laptop we can watch it.'*

This shows a non-caring attitude and no pride in one's work. If this is the kind of attitude before the sale, can you imagine what the service will be like after the sale? What kind of impression would you take of this person who walks in totally unprepared? Forget the impression, was he a good professional? Wouldn't he end up wasting the prospect's time? It is people like him, who not only don't end up selling, but also hurt the goodwill of the organization and the profession. He did not even care to prepare. A genuine mistake, once in a while, may be a different issue but this was a non-caring attitude. There is no substitute for hard work and preparation.

The more prepared the sales professional is, the greater the chance of making a sale. The more information we have about the prospect, the more prepared we can be to open and close the sale. Why? Because you can identify the possible need and suggest a suitable solution. Let us look at how we can prepare ourselves and what information could be helpful. This can also be called an 'informal fact-finding' exercise:

- Always check the client's website
- What are the values, vision and mission?
- What are the potential client's interests, hobbies, sports, etc.
- Is he a member of any clubs or fraternal organizations such as Rotary, Lions, Jaycees or the Round Table?
- What could be the compelling reason for them to start buying from you?
- Their credit rating and goodwill in the market?
- What is the decision-making process?

- Their business philosophy. How do they view their vendors? Is price the only consideration or do they look at long-term reliable relationships?
- What are their commitments to quality and its benchmarks?

Preparation also involves clarity of thought regarding the purpose of the meeting, which will determine:

1. What questions you need to ask?
2. What is the benefit to the prospect of dealing with you?

Is your true purpose to introduce yourself and open the door? Is it to get a trial order? Extend an existing order? The clarity in your mind will reflect in your presentation. The clearer you are, the more focused you will be and the greater the chance of closing the sale.

Selling Tools and Sales Aids

What is a sales aid or a tool to sell? Anything that assists you in making your sales presentation effective is a 'sales tool'. When people see, touch, feel and hear, there is no better evidence than experience! Their experience becomes your testimonial. All these are ways to reinforce the sales presentation or demonstrate the benefit of the product.

Tools and aids should be part of a good professional's sales kit. A professional salesperson should have a checklist. A pilot, even though he has flown thousands of hours, tallies everything, every time with the check-list before he takes off.

- It shows one's care and concern
- Quality consciousness
- Right performance
- It demonstrates professionalism
- It shows preparation.

What do you need in your presentation kit? These are little things which are not time consuming but they make a big difference. They only show your professionalism and concern for the prospect's time. A presentation kit can include:

1. Ample number of business cards
2. Brochures, flyers, the address of the company and product websites.
3. Product catalogue or brochure
4. Sample product (if it is easily portable) or other demo materials
5. Laptop, if you are going to make an electronic presentation
6. Presentation CDs – both audio and video
7. Copy of the direct mail if one was sent in advance
8. Fact sheets about your product/company (if different from the brochure)
9. A fact-finding check-list or questionnaire to establish need
10. Testimonial letters

Using a sales tools and demonstrations involves other sensory factors, and allows the prospect to participate in the buying process. Your product should appeal to all their senses; let them touch, feel and smell the product, as appropriate.

For example, have you ever noticed the aroma of warm bread as you enter a supermarket, or the visual appeal of many restaurants as you look in through the window when you walk past, or how when you are looking to buy a car, the salesperson will be very willing to take you for a test drive? As you become more attuned to the principles of selling, you'll notice more and more examples in your daily life that create good feelings without your even being aware of them at a conscious level. In some cases, such as, when you're given a free sample of perfume or of a household product in a supermarket, you'll go back with a feeling of pleasure and goodwill and not realize the underlying sales process that was taking place.

For sales tools to be effective, they must be self-explanatory. It means they should speak for themselves. They should be simple otherwise they detract. Always ensure that you optimize your time by making presentations to the decision maker. Many sales people keep making presentations without even finding out who the decision-maker is. No wonder their closing ratios go down.

Identify the People that Count

Since titles vary from company to company, there may be a total disconnect between the titleholder and the decision-maker. The titleholder and the authority holder may be totally different people and it is critical that you spend the majority of your time focused on the people that matter, and who can make the sale happen.

Good professionals establish the rules of the game before they start playing the game and they ask questions in order to gain a clear understanding. A good sales professional needs to know in advance who the key players in the decision-making process are. Those are the people he makes efforts to build relationships with. He needs to know:

- Who is the buyer?
- Who is the decision-maker?
- Who is the influencer?
- Who is the actual user?

One should not ask questions like 'Are you the decision-maker or what is your role in this purchase?' as they could be offensive because: a) he may feel small if he is not the decision-maker; b) just to feel important, he may give you wrong information; c) he may have ego hassles. Instead, seek to identify your decision-maker tactfully by asking:

- What is the decision-making process in your organization?
- Who else, besides you, would be involved in the decision-making process?'
- What is the buying criterion in your organization?
- What do you suggest?
- When would be a good time to touch base?
- What would you look for in a good supplier?
- How should we proceed from this point onward?
- What would you look for in a company that you would like to do business with?
- What would be your criteria for quality, service or the product?

♦ What would be a good response time in your opinion?

Without knowing the decision-making process and the degrees of influence of the different people in the customer's organization, you will be hampered in your ability to construct the best presentation and to satisfy the needs of the audience appropriately. For instance, sometimes the influencer/buyer may be a person different from the decision-maker. The decision-maker has the final say. The influencer generally may not have the authority to say 'yes' but he may be able to say 'no' to the purchase decision.

Sales people want to deal with decision-makers, but decision-makers don't want to deal with sales people unless they are also decision-makers. So, consider how you also represent yourself, so that you are efficient in how you focus on closing the sale and in keeping the buyer motivated to progress the discussions.

If the decision-making is done by a committee, then you'll need to find an ambassador for your product inside the buyer organization, and you'll need to coach him such that he can represent you authentically and with enthusiasm. He'll need to understand how to handle objections such as:

♦ Are the prices too high?
♦ Why should we do it now?
♦ What's the rush?
♦ What are the warranties/guarantees?
♦ What's the turnaround time?
♦ What's your credibility?

Making Presentations

Most sales professionals could multiply their sales if only they made great presentations. A great presentation cannot be fancy packaging alone, it needs to be substantive. It should be well-planned, structured, customer-focused and solution-oriented. It must move from a general presentation to specific needs and benefits because customers don't buy products and services, they only buy benefits and solutions.

Presentation Approach:

A good professional uncovers a need by:

1. Getting the prospect involved in a two-way transaction
2. Showing sincere interest in solving a problem
3. Earning trust
4. Asking questions
5. Active listening – verbal and non-verbal
6. Uncovering likes and dislikes, preferences and opinions
7. Creating areas of agreement
8. Re-phrasing and giving feedback to confirm understanding
9. Making some re-enforcing remarks or statements

It is important to get feedback because the salesperson comes to know if his presentation is on track or off track. It also engages and involves the prospect. Feedback also gives indicators as to what are the hot buttons of the prospect. It helps him uncover the needs and wants of the prospect. But most important – a salesperson must very carefully listen to what is being said and not being said. He will only get clues, provided he is an active listener and not a passive listener.

Presentation Tips

Do's	Don'ts
Go with a clear focus and identify your objective.	Be casual, careless and callous.
Take a deep breath, relax and speak clearly.	Be arrogant or have ego and prestige issues.
Be pleasant and behave naturally.	Exaggerate and make false promises.
Establish eye contact and smile.	Be pushy and pressurizing.
Be confident, sincere, honest and courteous.	Talk too much or be tense.
Be proud of your integrity, profession, product and company.	Manipulate or lie and conceal information.
Be prepared with all your selling tools and be knowledgeable about your product.	Doodle, stare, have shifty eyes or look distracted.
Keep your presentation to the point, sharp, crisp and brief.	Be offensive or defensive.
Communicate with both emotions and facts. Not just emotions.	Be drawn into an argument.
Give facts, not opinion and take notes carefully.	Sell unless you believe in what you sell.
Be sensitive to your client's needs and time constraints.	Try to close the sale without giving a strong benefit.
Convert features into benefits.	Compromise on values.
Analyze and learn from the questions prospects ask you.	Give unpleasant surprises – stick to your commitment.

Do's	Don'ts
Be prepared to handle objection.	Interrupt and joke unnecessarily.
Give the whole truth and make necessary disclosures.	Smoke or chew gum.
Set standards and benchmarks for your service and turnaround time. Speed is very important.	Play politics, bypass people.
Come through on your commitment and accept responsibility.	Ignore anyone, especially those who have an influence on decision-making.

Why is it important to make a statement or ask a question where the obvious answer is yes? 'Yes' is a form of agreement. The more 'yeses' you get during the presentation, the more agreement you have received. When you come to a close and, if the prospect has agreed with you so far, it will be difficult for him to disagree with you when you write up the order. His buying decision is being made step-by-step with every yes, mentally or verbally, which gets translated in the form of an order physically at the end.

The more 'yeses' you get, the easier it is for the prospect to make a positive decision.

14

PROSPECTING

❧

Prospecting is the lifeblood and key to success in sales. Daily prospecting is like sowing seeds every day. This ensures that you can harvest continuously. Sales professionals who get involved in too many activities, including sales presentations, either forget or don't have enough time to continuously prospect. That's when problems arise. They go into feast or famine mode. Even though it is very hard to tell when today's prospecting will show results, the process must continue. Regardless of how busy a person is today or how well they are doing, if they are looking to achieve good results in selling they must engage in prospecting every day.

This is because no matter what happens, there will always be a small percentage of your existing client base that will leave you; eventually, the business will dry up and at some point become non-existent. Your inflow and retention of prospects must be greater than the outflow. Only then can you grow.

What is the Difference between a Prospect and a Suspect?

Generally, for consumer goods, most people are suspects, but a few are prospects. How do you identify a prospect or convert a suspect into a prospect?

A prospect is a person who meets the following 3 criteria:

- A need for your product
- Ability to take a decision
- Money to buy your product

If any one of the above is missing, he is not a prospect.

Keep your focus on your target market: Be aware of your target group. Be aware that you cannot sell winter clothes in a warm climate. In selling, a salesperson must identify his prospect based on industry, age, occupation, income, etc.

To maintain a constant flow of new prospects, one needs to have a multiple approach, as one method cannot be relied upon exclusively. The salesperson, over a period of time, will develop their own level of comfort in the prospecting method. Good sales professionals always prioritize their prospects.

Sources of New Customers – we may get Prospects from:

1. News media
2. Competitors
3. Industry association memberships

4. Referrals from partners and existing clients
5. Networking through fraternal organizations
6. Telemarketing
7. Direct mailing
8. Advertisement
9. Cold calling
10. Websites and blogs
11. Trade shows.

Newspapers, magazines, companies or industrial groups announce promotions of new executives or new CEOs. I remember from my life insurance selling days that some people, very successfully, used to call the ones who were recently promoted. Regardless of the source of prospects, the methods of prospecting remain identical by and large. I shall just elaborate a few as follows:

METHODS OF PROSPECTING:

Direct Mail Marketing

I recall, in our office, when I was selling life insurance, we had one salesperson who was amongst the top producers. His marketing plan was very simple. He consistently sent ten mailers a day because he knew that 5 days later he would have to make phone calls to follow-up. Ten mailers per day cumulatively became fifty mailers a week. That means he made fifty phone calls a week. However, this was only for the first week. The cumulative impact will increase in the next week and even more in the following weeks. Gradually, over a period of time, with proficiency and good telephone handling skills, his ratio from mailers to appointment increased. Eventually, it resulted in making him one of the top salespersons in the company. The above example is a good one for marketing, consistency of follow-up and closing a sale. However, in the above example, if you notice there was no fancy strategy requiring special skills. The reason for success was commitment, self-discipline and consistency above all.

I also saw a behavior opposite to this. There was another salesperson who tried to replicate the top producers. He also started sending ten mailers a day. He made a very catchy introductory letter. In fact, after a few days he thought why do ten mailers a day, why not 1,000? He thought his business would multiply significantly, but the reverse actually happened. 2 major reasons: (1) It was feast or famine, either he sent too many, too few or none, (2) there was no follow-up or no consistency in the follow-up.

Just look at the difference in the 2 people. The second salesperson strategized with best intentions but faulty and inconsistent action. 1,000 letters a week without consistent follow-up died a natural death resulting in a loss. This clarifies that simply having good intentions doesn't get business. Good and consistent action brings business.

Being organized is important, but it is more important to be persistent and committed. There are people who are not the most organized ones but are committed and persistent, and this makes them successful. Consistent action in the right direction produces results.

Have a Direct Mail Marketing planning and tracking system, keeping in mind parameters such as age, income, occupation, location, etc. Decide the frequency and number of mailers to be sent and the enclosures (brochures, demo CDs, etc.) therein.

The most important thing is follow-up:

+ Without follow-up it is a losing proposition.
+ Consistency of follow-up is crucial because inconsistency means erratic follow-up and will not get desired results.
+ Unless the caller has rehearsed through role play properly, it will generate ill-will, forget getting any business.

Lastly, always determine how the outcome compared with your expectations.

Trade Shows

Trade shows can be a tremendous source of business. Professionals, who effectively work Trade Shows, keep the following in mind – they define very clear goals, as to what they want to accomplish through the show. Is it:-

+ Exposure to show presence,
+ Getting leads to follow-up later,
+ Close deals on the spot,
+ Distribute samples,
+ Organize a show, especially to generate interest or urgency to buy your product,
+ Just collect business cards to get possible qualified data, or
+ Re-establish contact with your existing customers.

No matter what your objective is, the ultimate aim remains to translate presentations into sales; hence, the approach should be to generate interest and close the sale in as few meetings as possible.

1. At the Trade Show, be proactive to generate traffic rather than wait for people to come by default. Keep in mind that proactive people do not sell products or services, they sell the benefits. They sell the sizzle not the steak. Trade Shows are not meant to socialize or chit-chat with people, but to establish new contacts with as many people as possible, in the shortest possible time, to optimize your investment of time and money.

2. Evaluate all the leads generated during the day. Translate them into hot, warm and cold leads on the same day, because by the next day you will not remember what is what. This will establish your priority of contacts.

3. Trade Shows will be fruitful only if the leads are followed-up immediately and professionally. Unfortunately, very few people and organizations do that. The follow-up of leads is crucial.

Existing Customers – The best source of new prospects is through referrals from existing customers

Also, if for any reason, the business stops or slows, one can always make an effort to go back to existing customers for additional business, provided you have built a relationship.

Ask your customers, why they bought your product, how satisfied are they, what were their needs, what benefit did they receive from buying your product? Then, ask yourself the same question.

If you have answers to these questions, then you have actually identified your prospects. All people who fall into this category are your prospects.

Cold Calling

While I was selling life insurance, I noticed that cold calling was not a very common way of prospecting, and I must say it was not one I enjoyed, yet there were some people who were top producers and used cold calling very effectively as a prospecting tool.

I recall one gentleman, who would invariably make it a practice to make four cold calls for every confirmed appointment. The reason was that he used to call the 2 adjoining places on each side, whether homes or offices. So, with 1 confirmed appointment he used to make 2 cold calls on either side of the confirmed appointment, fully prepared with a cold call script and benefit statement. Thus, he made the extra calls at no additional expense, little effort and better time management. Everybody would not be available or interested, but even if he got 1 new lead without much extra effort that contributed to making him of the top sales persons in his office.

Signature Presentation

A good sales professional creates a sixty-second grabber, or something called a 'trademark' or 'signature presentation'. This means that if you meet somebody at a get-together and they ask what you do, this is the thing to say. If you are going to give a long speech, you are going to lose out. In my case, if someone asks me what I do, I say,

'Mr Prospect, I am calling from XYZ Company. We have recently come up with a unique machine that can save you 20% of your running costs.'

If you have time for only 1 sentence, your sentence must be that which makes a person inquisitive. He should be saying, *'Tell me more about it.'* Now he is asking, you are not volunteering to speak.

What is your Market?

Develop your target market. Identify your prospect's profile. There is something called in-built or natural market. Another is called niche market. Niche market is our selected or chosen market.

The Natural Market

Project 100 – I learnt about the natural market when I was selling life insurance at MetLife. The day I joined, I was asked by the manager to make a list of 100 people I knew, whom I could call friends/relatives or acquaintances, and who were listed in my telephone diary, not the telephone directory. What was the logic behind contacting friends and relatives? Friends and relatives also have the need to protect their families by buying life insurance, and since we know them personally we don't have to establish our credibility from scratch. We have all the data, telephone numbers, addresses, etc., and most likely information on where they work, what they do for a living etc. Since, getting appointments is not difficult, they become the natural market.

I learnt that the following are the benefits of calling them:

1. Getting an appointment may be relatively easier than getting an appointment from outsiders or unknown people.

2. They are also buying these products from someone, so why not from you.

3. If they don't need your product today, at the very least they should know whom to contact when a need arises.

4. Hopefully the relationship will mean providing a better service.

5. Knowing your credibility, hopefully, they will give referrals much more easily even if they don't buy your product now. Good professionals build into their presentation a habit of acquiring enough referrals so that they don't run out of prospects.

Natural Market Prospecting Form – Friends/Relatives/Neighborhood

S. No.	Name	Address	Tele. No.	Called on	Status	
					Appnt. On	Next follow-up

The Niche Market – This is the market we choose to sell to:

Gradually, over a period of time, after experimenting with different professional, age groups and markets, I noticed that my closing ratio was higher in dealing with new home buyers for mortgage insurance. Very soon it became evident that if I concentrated more on this market, my return of time to investment was much higher. My proficiency became higher and it became much easier for me to sell mortgage insurance because I had developed a unique presentation which resulted in a higher closing ratio.

Approach

No matter what your prospecting method is, the basic principles do not change, whether it is through telephone, cold calls or through direct mail. The basic approach remains identical. The guidelines as are follows:

1. Your opening statement must grab the prospect's attention.
2. Get to the point.
3. Your opening statement must be a benefit statement.
4. Always put yourself in the receiver's position as you develop your script.
5. Anticipate response from the receiver's perspective.

No one method of prospecting should be relied upon, a good salesperson opens many doors. A good sales professional always prioritizes their prospects into:

Hot	Warm	Cold
These are the ones who are excited about your product and are likely to do business in the near future.	These are the ones who are the fence sitters. They want the product but are non-committal, yet they don't want to say no because they don't want to lose out on something good.	These are the people who are not excited or sold on your product. They are totally indifferent or resistant and require a lot of effort to be sold.

Since there is only so much time, an effective professional is result-oriented, prioritizes and spends 80% of time on the hot leads, 15% on the warm leads and 5% on the cold leads. This is because 80% of the revenue comes from the hot leads.

Referrals are a great way of prospecting.

15

REFERRALS AND TESTIMONIALS

Referrals are an effective method of prospecting which allows the sales professional to open new doors on favorable grounds. The existing client gives referrals because he has enough confidence in the salesperson's integrity or competence that he is willing to put his credibility on the line. By borrowing this credibility, the sales professional turns a cold call into a meaningful chance to make a sale.

- Do you get referrals?
- How often do you get referrals (is it 1 out of 10 or 1 out of 20)
- What do you say to get referrals?

Asking for Referrals

Make asking for referrals a part of your presentation. In order to get referrals we must do the following:

+ Establish good rapport with the client.
+ Have a satisfied client.
+ Know how to ask for referrals.
+ Be proactive.

In case, a person is hesitant to give referrals, the salesperson must find out the reason for the hesitation. Getting referrals is a matter of earning them, because referrals put the referring party at risk. Hence, the only way to get referrals is to have established trust. Referrals don't happen automatically. They have to be actively solicited. They are like your grade in a test. They tell you how well you have performed.

A sales professional had a great way for asking for referrals. He used to say, *'Mr Prospect, I find that caring people, whenever they find something good, want their close friends and family members to benefit from it as they themselves have benefited.'*

Other approaches are:

1. 'If your friend found something of phenomenal value or a great doctor, would you not want him to tell you about it, so that you could also benefit, if and when the need arises?'
2. 'If your friend or close relative walked in right now, would you be embarrassed to introduce me to them?'

3. 'Which 3 people who come to your mind are in a position similar to yours, who could benefit from our services?'

Good professionals not only get referrals they also give referrals. Referrals are one of the smartest ways of prospecting. The reasons are:

1. It is the fastest way to leverage and borrow credibility from your satisfied customers without having established any of your own, because:
   a. By opening the door for you, the referred party extends a courtesy to his friend.
   b. People feel if something is good enough for their friend it must be good for them too. Why miss out?
   c. It establishes instant confidence, trust and reduces suspicions.
   d. It reduces the risk for the prospect and brings predictability.
   e. It also brings curiosity, 'Why is everybody buying it?'
2. By using a referral's name a possible cold prospect might turn into a receptive listener. It does not guarantee a sale but it opens the door and allows you to get a foothold.
3. If the referral likes the solution offered by you and decides to accept your recommendation, he would thank the friend who referred you. The reverse is also true.

In order to get referrals, you must:

a. Earn the right to ask for a referral which can happen only if you have done a great job and delighted your customer.

b. You must know how to ask for the referral.

c. Ask – Most sales people don't ask for referrals, which is walking away from potential business.

Never ask for a referral by saying, *'Do you know of anyone who would be interested in buying this product/service.'* 99% of the time the likely answer would be 'no'.

A professional way of asking would be, *'Mr Prospect, just the way your business grows by word of mouth from satisfied clients, so does mine. I would assume you are totally satisfied, aren't you.'*

Chances are the answer would be 'yes', since he has just bought your product.

'Who are your 3 closest friends that I could talk to regarding this? Or who are the 3 friends you play golf with or socialize with at the club'?

This is the time the sales professional should be ready expectantly with a pen and paper, to write down the names and telephone numbers. If he is not ready, chances are he will not receive them.

Another good way of getting referrals, upon completion of a sale to a customer's satisfaction, is to ask permission to take a very short survey by saying something like this: *'Mr Customer, would you mind if I shared your opinion of our services with our management?'* If the customer is satisfied, chances are that he will not mind it at all.

Here are the questions:

1. What 3 things did we do right that helped you decide on our product?

a.

b.

c

2. What 3 things could we do to improve our services?

    a.

    b

    c.

3. What could we do to earn the right to get referrals from you?

    (Either he would say that you have earned the right or he would say do this and earn the right.)

    a.

    b.

    c.

4. Which 3 people do you have in mind to refer us to?

    a.

    b.

    c.

Always **seek permission** to use the person's name by saying, *'Is it okay if I mention your name as a reference?'* Try to get as much information (name, address, telephone numbers and type of business) of the party referred, it will only help you prepare better for the next appointment. Keep the person who provided the referral informed of the status of the contact made by you. Regardless of the outcome, always send a 'thank you' note appreciating the reference. If you do end up finalizing a business, it is all the more reason that a courteous thank you be sent.

Some people establish contact with the party to whom they are referred either in writing or by phone or both.

A strong referral is considered a hot lead, and if not acted upon immediately it turns cold; hence, the probability of doing business goes down.

Frequently Asked Questions

What if I have not been able to establish a rapport with the customer? Or somehow we are not able to get our personalities in sync at all, or if my company is not providing good service or products. Would I still be able to get referrals and should I ask? The answer is: No.

You won't get referrals and you should not even ask, for 3 very clear reasons:

1. The client is not sold on you.
2. You haven't earned the right to ask.
3. If you wouldn't buy your company's product, you have no right to sell it either.

Your remedy is to either upgrade your company's product or service and make your organization a quality organization, or work with a quality organization.

Your current satisfied customers can become a tremendous source of referrals and testimonials. Each sale made is your success story for a future sale.

Testimonials are what give authenticity to a sales professional when the prospect needs a proof of the claim made by the salesperson. Their word of mouth is the biggest service of PR and advertising that you could receive without any out of pocket payment for it.

TESTIMONIALS

A testimonial really gives confidence to the prospect who mentally tells himself:

*   If they could trust the seller, so can I.
*   They must have done their due diligence.
*   If the products are good enough for them I'm sure they would be good for me too.
*   They must have been satisfied that's why they gave a testimonial letter.

These testimonials are genuine with names, addresses and telephone numbers, they are not anonymous. If anyone wants to check your credibility they are free to do so. It is crucial that from every satisfied client one should endeavor to take written testimonials to make future prospecting easier.

How do you obtain a Testimonial Letter?

The incorrect way is to just ask for one. To this the client replies, *'I'll send it to you.'* Do you think you will ever get a letter? – Never! Why? This is because your client's and your priorities are very different. He may just forget.

The following approach worked well for me when I was in the insurance sales industry. I would do the following:

1. Confirm that the client is totally satisfied.
    'Mr . . . , do I take it that you are totally satisfied with the solution that we have provided you? It takes care of your need, doesn't it?' Generally, the answer was 'yes'.

2. 'Could I use your name in case somebody would want to talk to a satisfied client?' Client, 'Yes.'

3. 'Just to make it easy I can draft a testimonial letter with your approval or any amendments, you can have it photocopied on your letterhead, would that be OK? I will bring it personally as I will be in your neighborhood anyways.'

Now, who drafts the letter? You do! Obviously, you will make yourself look good, but do not exaggerate or be flowery. Be conservative, factual and honest. The purpose of the letter is to convey the reliability and trustworthiness of the sales professional.

A testimonial letter ought to bring out more of the benefit received by the purchaser than how good the sales person or the company was, because people are looking for a benefit.

During the days when I was selling life insurance, I had a client who passed away, within a few days of signing the application. As part of our training we were taught that whenever a death claim is processed and a cheque issued, it should never be sent in the mail to the client, but always delivered personally.

This is because the death of a loved one is a very emotionally disturbing time and all the friends and relatives come to sympathize, some genuine, some out of formality. The life insurance person is the only one who goes to the bereaved spouse with a cheque. This cheque represents food on the table, education for the kids, medicine in case of sickness and a roof over their heads. Sympathies or sympathy-givers do not provide any of these things.

The following is the testimonial letter of a case that happened, which I used for almost a decade. The letter was addressed to my manager:

Dear _____,

Mr Shiv Khera, visited our home on . . . (Date) and recommended a mortgage insurance policy on the home that I and my husband bought recently. We both thought that this was a waste of money, and we really didn't need any insurance. Reluctantly, we signed the application and gave him a cheque of $27,000/-.
Unfortunately, my husband passed away within a few days of signing the application.
Today, Mr Khera has brought a cheque of $63,000/- which will pay off my mortgage and I can stay peacefully in my own home.
He was the only one who came with a cheque, while the rest came with sympathies. I cannot thank him enough for his professionalism and timely help.

Regards
J.S.

A testimonial letter represents authenticity because it is given by people who have a face, an address and a phone number. It represents a statement of proof and gives tremendous credibility. It substantiates your work. Words are cheap and many times prospects doubt words, but written and signed documents are trusted more. Hence, testimonial letters are powerful tools to get rid of objections in advance.

Caution: Make sure that you do not get involved in name-dropping or bragging and boasting about yourself. That sounds like self-praise and it's a turn off and creates doubt. Most people respect and respond very warmly to humility.

16

CALL RELUCTANCE AND TELEPHONE CALLING

Call Reluctance Leads to Inaction

Call reluctance comes from a fear of being rejected; and whenever a person is rejected, a person's self-esteem goes down and he feels de-motivated. Winners recognize that success is achieved not in the absence of problems, but through overcoming them.

> Intention without action = zero result
> Action without direction = zero result

Nobody wants to know what you will do. We all want to know what you did do.

Just like iron gets rusted with disuse, stagnant water decays and loses its purity and a lack of physical exercise weakens the body; likewise, inaction weakens people mentally. Call reluctance and the lack of desire to pursue sales opportunities leads to inaction. Approximately:

> **Nobody wants to know what you will do. We all want to know what you did do.**

- 50% salespeople quit after the first rejection
- 60% quit after the second rejection
- 70% quit after the third rejection
- 80% quit after the fourth rejection

Only 20% of people go beyond the fourth call and 80% of sales are made around the fifth closing attempt. No wonder 20% of people are making 80% of the sales.

To face rejection in professional selling takes a lot of courage. Many people have wishbones, but what they lack is a backbone!

If a farmer does not sow in the right season, he will not have any harvest at reaping time. Similarly, if a salesperson doesn't meet/call prospects, he will have no sale. This is commonsense. **No calls = No Sales.**

People who wait for things to happen never get anywhere.

Abraham Lincoln once said, 'Things may come to those who wait, but only the things left by those who hustle.'

Using the Telephone to Make Appointments

Getting appointments through the effective use of telephones can save a lot of time and also be cost effective. Imagine if you are trying to meet someone without an appointment, and you find out that you have traveled many miles only to be informed that the person is not there nor is the decision-maker.

Some people shy away from using the phone for whatever reason and take the simpler, but often less effective approach, of sending a fax or an e-mail. To overcome telephone call reluctance have a question and answer session in your mind:

- What is the worst that can happen?
- If the worst happens, so what?
- If I didn't call, I would have been rejected without any effort, anyway.
- If I get rejected, so what? At least I had the courage to make an effort.

Sometimes, sales people are not able to talk to the prospect as the phone is answered by the secretary.

How to Bypass the Secretary or Gatekeeper

Keep in mind that this person's job is to screen unwanted calls and relieve the pressure on the boss. It is her job to help increase productivity and to ensure that the boss only meets those he wants or needs to see. Her job is to comply with those requirements. Here are some effective ways that will increase your chances of reaching the boss.

Once you've made the call, if the secretary asks, *'What is it about?'*

The answer is, *'Could I speak to Mr XYZ please? This is about a cost saving of 20%.'*

Now analyze this statement. If there is something that could genuinely save 20%, it is certainly worthwhile for the boss. Also, note that if the boss comes to know later on that he wasn't put through, guess what would happen!

If it is a call given by a referral, you can say, '*Mr Prospect, so and so benefited from our services and thought that you could also do the same. He gave your name and suggested I call you. Could I possibly see you sometime next week, would you prefer Monday or Tuesday?*' The alternate choice method or formula is considered old and obsolete, but in my experience it is one of the best ways to approach a person. It is psychologically very effective.

When speaking to the secretary

1. Introduce yourself clearly, by name and company.
2. Don't avoid her questions or mumble and fumble. You have to impress her as well.
3. Be pleasant and courteous, but don't try to be pompous.
4. It is preferable not to ask 'How are you today?' because it sounds phoney. Don't make it a social call. Be precise and to the point.
5. Don't say it is a personal call, because that would be a lie; you lose your credibility and it irritates the prospect.
6. Don't ask for person by his first name.
7. Don't read your telephone sales script, because people can tell it is canned.
8. Make your point and then remain silent for a few seconds. Silence puts the pressure on the secretary to put you through.

Upon fixing the appointment, immediately reconfirm it in writing. Send an e-mail or fax. Don't call and reconfirm with the client especially if it is the first appointment. You may call the secretary and leave a word that she can note it down in her appointment book and remind him.

Whenever a prospect receives a cold call, whether in person or through the phone, immediately some questions come to their mind – who is calling, why is he calling, why is he calling me specifically, why should I talk, and what's in it for me?

This is where a strong opener is very crucial. You need to make a benefit statement which is authentic or a claim that you can substantiate. For example – 'Mr Prospect, I am calling from XYZ Company. We have recently come up with a unique machine that can save you 20% of your running costs. I am sure you would be interested in the savings, wouldn't you?'

(Caution: You should be able to substantiate the claim of 20%.)

Asking a question which benefits the prospect immediately gets his attention.

Be sensitive and cognizant of the fact that when you call a prospect your call could be interrupting something important, encroaching on a person's time and possibly his priority. Your presentation at this time may not only be discourteous but ill-mannered too. Such an intrusion may become an irritation.

The question is how do you bring softness and politeness in such situations? If you notice that the approach given below shows humility, and of course, there should be politeness in the tone of voice. This is easily done by always seeking permission in the following manner:

- Do you have a minute to talk?, or
- Is it a good time to talk?
- If this is not a good time, what would be a good time for me to call? (Be careful that you ask this only if the tone of voice is receptive, and not brisk. If you are not sensitive, it would irritate the prospect even more.)

If you are making a phone call to a prospect for the first time, you need to ask yourself: what is the purpose of the phone call – is it an introduction, a presentation or to make an appointment?

Your approach and rapport-building would vary based on your primary objective. A cardinal rule for phone presentations or for a face-to-face presentation is that you should not speak more than 35-40 seconds without getting a response. The response may be a 'Yes' or 'No', or an acknowledgement, it doesn't matter. However, it is important to get the prospect involved through a proper questioning technique, every 15 seconds.

In preparing a telephone prospecting script, keep the following points or steps in mind in the same order:

1. Short introduction – your name and company
2. Permission to talk
3. Benefit statement opener
4. Frame your questions where the prospect's response can only be a 'yes'.
5. Be prepared to handle 3 most common objections.

Ideas Important for Effective Telephone Skills:

1. Prepare your data 1 day in advance for your phone calls.
2. Fix a specific time every day to make your phone calls.
3. Fix the number of calls per hour.
4. Ensure you achieve your hourly target (Don't play games with yourself.)
5. Prepare your script in advance.
6. Practice your telephone script till it is internalized.
7. Your voice should be pleasant without being over-friendly.
8. Your positive attitude reflects in your tone.
9. Your conviction and belief in your products is reflected in your voice.
10. Be confident but polite.
11. Speak at a pace which is neither too fast nor too slow. Too fast shows nervousness, too slow is irritating.
12. Make sure you only make a presentation to the decision-maker.
13. Practice courtesy and politeness with whoever answers the phone regardless of whether they are decision-makers or not.
14. Calling at the right time increases your chances in getting to talk to decision-makers.
15. Always make note of your conversation. This helps you follow up and convert a cold call into a hot call. Otherwise, every call will remain a cold call.
16. Don't let gossip mongers and other interruptions distract you and waste time.

17. Don't let negative people pull you down by telling you how many rejections they got.

18. Have faith in the law of averages.

19. Keep yourself motivated by thinking positive thoughts and reading your goals every day.

20. Keep targeting for small successes every day.

21. Show enthusiasm and be energetic – it reflects in your voice.

22. Make sure you address people by their proper titles, e.g. Doctor, Professor, etc.

23. Make sure you pronounce people's names correctly. If you are not sure, ask, 'Am I pronouncing your name correctly?' People appreciate your asking them rather than hearing their name pronounced wrongly.

24. Always address people by their title – Mr or Ms. Don't call people by their first name without their permission unless they are junior to you in age or otherwise. Calling people by their first name is a privilege given to you by them.

25. Practice courtesy by always asking permission before you start making an opening statement.

26. Keep your telephone call short, brief and to the point.

27. Preferably, try to talk to the telephone operator or receptionist and see if the prospect is in the office, and check what would be a good time to call.

28. You could follow up your telephone message with an e-mail.

Approach

Prepare yourself with some strong and powerful openers. Try them out. Rehearse and practice them keeping in mind that gimmicks and tricks are short-lived and make you lose credibility. In our training process we use the following principles:

For example: 'Mr X, do you have a minute to talk?'

If the prospect says 'yes' then our telemarketer goes ahead and makes the presentation. If not, they ask, 'What is a good time to reach you?', or 'Can I call you later?' You ask this question because:

- It is only courteous to get permission before making a presentation.
- Is it fair to impose on a person's time without permission?
- What if, it is not a good time and you start making a presentation; it would not only be discourteous but irritating to the other person. How many times have you had a telemarketer call and start making a presentation not bothering about whether you have a headache or heart attack or somebody is sick in your family? Is that a good time to talk? Obviously not!

If the prospect says OK, then you make your presentation keeping in mind that you have to get his attention within the first 10 seconds. It is all about the impact of your opening sentence and nothing much other than that. Keep in mind that you have only 1 chance. Here is what to say:

'Mr Prospect, I am calling from XYZ Company. We have recently come up with a unique machine that can save you

20% of your running costs. I am sure you would be interested in the savings, wouldn't you?' (The same question has been repeated for the purpose of giving you an illustration or an example. Please create your own questions based on your product and benefits.)

If you analyze this question, the only answer to this question, should be a 'yes'. The way it is phrased it has to be a 'yes'. Who or how could anyone say 'no' as an answer to this question. It would be a rarity if somebody does. Are we catering to this person? No, we are not catering to the 0.01% who say 'no'. We are not looking for this person, because, anyway, he may not be a prospect. However, just to give him the benefit of doubt we ask, 'Mr X, why do you feel that way?' This question in a way encourages him to revaluate his own answer, and if he realizes his mistake, he may correct his answer. It could be that he has had a bad day or fought with somebody and he is not interested.

If you are in the real estate business you might have some property tax records from the municipal corporation, which is public information. You might say something to the effect:

'Mr ABC, I have your tax records in front of me, of X property, I might have a potential buyer in your area. I just thought I will check with you in case you want to encash it and make some profit on your investment.'

Fixing Appointments on the Telephone

First Approach:
'Mr ABC asked me to give you a call and share some ideas that have been profitable to people such as yourself. Could we possibly meet next week Monday or Tuesday?'

Second Approach:

'I read your name in the newspaper regarding a promotion/the stand you have taken. Could I possibly meet you next week to share some ideas that will be profitable to your organization. What would be better – next Monday or Tuesday?'

Third Approach

'I want to thank you for the courtesy you have extended. In order for me to suggest appropriate solutions, which day would be better to meet – Monday or Tuesday?'

Fourth Approach

'For an existing client: Mr ABC, I see you have a photocopier which is 6 years old. We have an exchange program to provide you a new machine which will save you 20%, based on your current usage. When would it be better for you to meet – next Monday or Tuesday?'

Fifth Approach

'Mr ABC, this is Mr DEF calling from XYZ Company, I sent a letter to you along with a CD, sharing some cost saving ideas that have been useful for many organizations like yours. Could we possibly meet up next week, either Monday or Tuesday?'

Handling Specific Objections

*   *'I am not interested.'*
    'Mr ABC, I can understand you're not interested in something that you haven't had a look at so far. Without any obligation, may I share with you next week, how

companies like yours have benefited. What would be more convenient, Monday or Tuesday?'

* 'I don't have the time – Send me some information.'
  Mr ABC, I would be happy to send you the brochure and information which would probably take you an hour or 2 to read. However, if I stop by for fifteen minutes next week, that will save you a lot of time and I could share with you the benefits. What would be more convenient, next Monday or Tuesday?'

* 'My purchase manager takes the decision.'
  'Mr ABC, Thanks for your help. Could I kindly have his/her number so I can speak to him/her?'

Telephone Messages

Leaving a message on the voice mail, could be a double-edged sword. But under no circumstances leave a message more than twice. If the phone is not answered the second time when you call, hang up. Calling time and again and leaving a message comes across as nagging.

The following is a poor example: 'Mr Prospect, my name is XYZ with ABC Company. We are the number 1 providers of high quality product/services in this sector. I am calling to get together with you to discuss how we can meet your requirements. When you get a chance please call me on ABC number.'

A polite person may return the call, but otherwise, the salesperson has not really given the prospect any reason to call back.

Another example: 'Mr Prospect, this is XYZ calling to share some ideas that could be mutually profitable. When you get a chance, please call me on this number.' This approach gets the prospect's attention because it gives him a good reason to call back as he used the term 'mutually profitable'.

Analyzing the second example, it does not guarantee that the phone call will be returned, but of the 2, it has a greater chance of receiving the phone call because it makes the prospect curious. He could possibly want to know what would be mutually profitable. Even though the salesperson says 'mutually profitable', the prospect is thinking about what is profitable to him. The next question that comes is, did the salesperson lie anywhere? The answer is no. He was totally ethical and professional and the idea could be mutually profitable. Curiosity makes the prospect want to pick up the phone and talk to the salesperson. As a sales professional, you want to open the door in order to establish credibility.

There is an old saying that: 'You can take the horse to the water but you can't make him drink.' Nowadays, there is a new twist to the old saying – while taking the horse to the water, make sure you make him thirsty. How do you make a horse thirsty? Put a little salt in his food and he will become thirsty. That way when he gets to the water he is thirsty enough to drink and he drinks. Just as drinking is the natural outcome of being thirsty, in the selling profession closing is the natural outcome of a good presentation. The more curious the buyer is, the more he wants to know. The more he wants to know, the greater the opportunity for the salesperson to bring value addition.

A big success is the result of or accumulation of many little successes. I have seen some sales professionals very successfully, use the following approach 'Mr Prospect, I am X calling from ABC Company. I had a question which, probably, you are the most qualified to answer. I would appreciate a call back from you. My number is ....'

Analyze the above approach. If I was selling life insurance and I left such a message for the prospective decision-maker by saying I had a question that probably he is the most qualified person to answer, what would happen?

- It raises his curiosity.
- The question that comes to the prospect's mind is, 'What is it that I am the most qualified person for?' The prospect would want to know!

When the prospect returns the call, the salesperson's approach would be 'since you are heading XYZ department, I felt you are the most qualified person to ask.

'We have recently come up with a unique group insurance program that can save you 10% of your present costs. I am sure you would be interested in the savings, wouldn't you?

The most obvious answer to this question is 'yes'. It still gives you an opportunity to open the door.

The same principles apply to e-mails as apply to voice mail. People are bombarded with e-mails. On the subject title you need to write 'I have a question' rather than writing the actual subject.

'Since you are heading XYZ department, I felt you are the most qualified person to ask. We have recently come up with a unique machine that can save you 20% of your running costs. I am sure you would be interested in the savings, wouldn't you?

Factors that raise a prospect's curiosity are:

- The unknown
- Thought provoking information
- Something newsworthy
- Value propositions
- Incomplete information
- Gain of unknown benefit
- Prevention of unknown loss

Another approach – 'Mr Prospect, our office did a study in the last 3 weeks and came up with a report that highlights some serious problems that could affect productivity in your organization.'

If the above is the opening sentence received by the decision-maker, what's the first thing that comes into his mind? 'What problem could affect our productivity?' Wouldn't he want to know immediately? The curiosity must be strong enough to prompt the prospect to invite you and then of course as a good professional, you must talk sense. Otherwise, it would be irritating and you and your organization would lose credibility. Keep in mind: our object is to open the door and build credibility, thereby turning it into a mutually profitable relationship.

One Can Raise Curiosity and Yet Maintain Integrity

Credibility is the level of trustworthiness and helps open the door. Sometimes, people question how you can build credibility unless you open the door. My answer is that they are mutually inclusive. The moment you open the door and the way you open the door, starts building or depleting credibility. Whether we like it or not, we have to accept that all past negative experiences from previous vendors will make the buyers' skeptical till you prove otherwise. The basic perception of a salesperson is that they are not trustworthy and they will do anything to make a sale, till it is proven otherwise. A good sales professional should not be deterred because of this perception.

Why is Accurate Record Keeping Important?

* Your phone-contact ratio shows if you are calling at the right time of the day or week. For example, accountants should not be called during tax season. Attorneys are generally called after 4.30 pm. Similarly, with experience you can develop your own schedule to call.
* Contact-appointments ratio show your telephone skills. Also, how well you bypass the secretary.
* Call-presentation ratio shows your ability to speak to the decision-maker. (You only make a presentation to the decision-maker and nobody else.)
* Your presentation-sales ratio shows your closing ratio or your selling skills.

Unless we are aware of our selling skills as above we will never be able to reach our goals in life.

17

RULES FOR LETTER WRITING

Start with a very strong opening headline, because if the headline is not attractive, people will not read further. This means, **a headline is an advertisement to an advertisement**, or an announcement.

1. Address from the prospective buyer's point of view.
2. Focus on 1 major idea at a time. Be specific. (Don't beat around the bush.)
3. Go with a logical sequence.
4. Use bullet points to emphasize benefits. Use testimonials for credibility and give proof of your claims.
5. Keep your letters short and brief, preferably half-page by and large. It is better not to exceed 1 page unless totally necessary (keep in mind: your prospect will read so much only if you have grabbed his attention with the opening

statement). Write short paragraphs both for openers and closers.

6. Always proofread and spell-check your letter very carefully from the receiver's perspective.

7. Personalize your letter by checking out the name of the prospect and spelling it correctly.

8. Give them a strong reason to talk to you or see you. Make it compelling.

9. Include a brochure if it helps your chances of making the sale. (A brochure is a selling tool. But keep in mind that the brochure does not replace you.)

10. Don't promise something that you cannot do.

11. Close your letter with a call to action, either from your prospect's side or your side. Adhere to any commitments that you may make, but give some breathing time before the follow-up.

12. You can ask him to take an action. (Example: please acknowledge this letter. They may or may not acknowledge, but that is immaterial.)

13. Informing them that you will be taking an action. (Example: I shall call you within 3 to 5 days from now. Always specify a specific time period during which you will follow-up. Don't leave it open such as – 'I shall call you later to follow-up.' These are vague and loose statements. (This does not show seriousness.)

SAMPLE LETTERS

Letter 1 – A Sample Pre-approach

A real estate sales person could use the following letter:

Date: -----------------

Name
Title
Address

Dear Mr/Mrs/Ms........................,

Are you tired of looking for office space?
Now you can get office space that you can be proud of and which doesn't cost you an arm and a leg. We have recently built a new office space at.........I shall call you next week or..........and share with you the business opportunity that could be mutually profitable, similar to what we have done for XYZ Company.

Regards,
ABC

Letter 2 – A Sample Pre-approach

Date: ----------------

Name
Title
Address

Dear Mr/Mrs/Ms......................,

Your name was mentioned by.............saying that your company has reached a new benchmark/or your name was mentioned in the newspaper achieving new benchmarks. May I congratulate you on your achievement?

With this letter I introduce myself saying that: Mr........................., I am calling from XYZ Company. We have recently come up with a unique machine that can save you 20% of your running costs. I am sure you would be interested in the savings, wouldn't you?

I shall call you next Monday to schedule an appointment and share ideas that have been helpful to people like you.

I look forward to speaking with you next week.

Regards,
ABC

Letter 3 – A Sample Pre-approach

Date: ----------------

Name
Title
Address

Dear Mr/Mrs/Ms....................,

Most decision-makers feel that if their people have a better attitude, their team work and productivity goes up. I am sure, you feel the same way.

I shall call you next Monday morning to schedule an appointment and share ideas that have been helpful to people like you.

Looking forward to speaking with you next week.

Regards,
XYZ

Letter 4 – A Sample Follow-up

Date: ----------------

Name
Title
Address

Dear Mr/Mrs/Ms....................,

Thank you for the courtesy extended during our recent meeting. As discussed, enclosed is additional information that could help you enhance your productivity through our product/service.

I will call you next Monday to schedule a meeting or answer any questions you may have.

Regards,
XYZ

Letter 5 – A Sample Follow-up

Date: ----------------

Name
Title
Address

Dear Mr/Mrs/Ms......................,

Thank you for the courtesy extended and the opportunity to meet with you. As promised, enclosed are the following pieces of information:

1.
2.
3.

I will call you next Monday to schedule a meeting or answer any questions you may have.

Regards,
XYZ

Letter 6 – A Sample Referral

Date: ----------------

Name
Title
Address

Dear Mr/Mrs/Ms.....................,

This is just a note to thank you for referring XYZ. I shall keep you posted of the outcome.

Thank you again for your help and consideration. If I can assist you in any manner, please do not hesitate to call.

Regards,
ABC

Letter 7 – A Sample for a Reconfirmation in Writing

Date: ----------------

Name
Title
Address

Dear Mr/Mrs/Ms.....................,

Thank you for the courtesy extended. I am looking forward to seeing you on .... (Date), at.......... (Time). If there is any change, I will appreciate receiving a call from you. If I don't hear from you: I will take this appointment as confirmed.

Regards,
XYZ

Letter 8 – A Sample Testimonial Letter

Date: ----------------

Name
Title
Address

To whom it may concern
or
Addressed to the Salesperson

Dear..............,

This is just a note to thank you for your courteous and professional service. Your integrity has inspired a lot of confidence in your company and your solutions have enhanced my business significantly/saved me a significant amount in terms of money.
I would recommend your service to anyone. Please feel free to give my office number to anyone who wants to reconfirm my experience with you.

Regards,
XYZ

18

QUESTIONS ARE THE ANSWERS

Selling is not Telling, it is Asking Questions

This is because questions engage the other person, give the sales professional clues to steer his presentation and generally puts him in the driver's seat.

A good sales presentation should not be a monologue, but rather an opportunity to ask the prospect a number of valuable questions. After you make your brief introduction, you want to find out whether the prospect has a need for your product. Before asking questions the salesperson must earn the right to ask questions by taking permission, 'In order to provide you the right solution, do you mind if I ask you a few questions?' If you analyze this question, it gives a reason to ask a question and seeks permission. The reason is given before seeking permission because it shows courtesy and humility. It lowers the guard of the potential buyer because it takes the threatening or interrogative aspect out of it. It is important because, if a question is asked without giving a reason first, it might sound offensive and interrogative and the other person might become defensive. If I just said, 'Do you mind if I ask a few questions?', this question asks permission but gives no reason. It is better than asking questions without permission. However, the prospect may sometime still be uncomfortable because he has not been given a reason.

There are 2 kinds of questions – **open-ended** and **close-ended.** Open-ended questions are those that cannot be answered with a simple 'Yes' or 'No'. **These are questions beginning with – Why, When, Where, Who, How and What.** They have to be answered by giving information. Examples of open-ended questions:

- How do you plan to use this in your day-to-day operations?
- Which 3 elements are most critical to you from the utility perspective?
- What are your major requirements in the office?
- Where do you plan to use this?
- Please help me understand how . . . ?
- Where are you going?
- What time is it?

A close-ended question can be answered in 'Yes' or 'No'. Such questions only give you confirmation but no information. For example:

1. Can I help you?   No
2. Can I have an ice-cream?   Yes

3. Are you looking to buy something today? Yes/No

The old saying, 'Selling is not telling', remains true and timeless.

Just because questions are important and need to be asked, it does not mean that sales people know **how to ask or what to ask**. If the **how** and **what** to ask are missing, one can be sure that they are not going to get the right answer, and for that matter the prospect may even be antagonized. Hence, one needs to know not only **'what to do'**, but also what **'not to do'**. A doctor has a dual approach – preventive and curative. He gives one medicine or multi-vitamins to build immunity and another medicine to get rid of the infection. Similarly, a salesperson needs to not only increase his chances of closing the sale, but reduce the risk of failure. Effective and skillful questioning helps in making the prospect respond favorably. No matter what you sell, selling principles are fundamental and applied universally.

Questions are important because, they:

1. Put you in charge or in control of the presentation
2. Uncover the need
3. Identify the decision-maker
4. Bring out objections
5. Find out the buying motive
6. Can bring more agreements
7. Can convert a monologue into a dialogue
8. Can engage and involve the prospect in the conversation

9. Help to bring a disagreement into the open rather than have the prospect disagree in silence, which could be detrimental to the sale.

Good sales professionals keep their questions simple and to the point. They have a logical sequence of questions from general to specific. Since, this is so important, I repeat – **Always take permission before asking questions. Keep the tone of your voice humble and polite.**

Keeping the conversation positive as you build the relationship

It goes without saying that the questioning process should be designed to build the relationship and to elicit information.

Don't ask questions which might sound like you are questioning the buyer's intelligence.

*   Is increasing productivity important to you? or,
*   Is cost saving important to you?

Now, such questions sound like no-brainers, somebody has to be stupid to say 'No' to them.

We should ask questions that gets a person thinking, such as:

*   Have you ever calculated the cost of a machine running 40% slower than what is available today?
*   Have you ever wondered what 30% savings in turnaround time would mean to your customer service?
*   Can you imagine the exposure that you have if your data remains unprotected?

+ Can you imagine the risk to your credibility if your client's confidential information remains unprotected?

All the above questions are disturbing and can get the buyer thinking about what can be improved in his operation today. Asking questions to clarify a need requires a lot of tact and skill; the words we use are very important. We don't ask questions like:

+ What's your problem?
+ What do you mean?
+ Can you explain yourself?
+ Can or may I have your business?

The above questions can be offensive even with a polite tone. Instead, we could use the following:

+ Would you mind elaborating a little?
+ Could you clarify with an example?
+ Could I request you to think aloud?
+ In your opinion, what would be an ideal solution?
+ I am a little embarrassed to ask but in order to provide the right solution, may I just ask . . .
+ Just to clarify my thinking, is . . . what you meant?
+ Forgive me, but I need to ask . . . in order to do the right procedure for you.
+ Do you think it might be fair to ask if . . . ?
+ Do you mind if I ask what seems to be holding you back?
+ What seems to be your concern?
+ On a scale of 1 to 10 where do you think you stand

in your decision-making? Suppose he says, 'I am at 3,' your follow-up question right away could be, 'What can I do to help you come to 8 or 9?'

- Mr Prospect, is there something that I have done that is bothering you. Or, if there is something I have done inadvertently that might have offended you, I would be happy to apologize.

If you notice the above questions, they all have something in common. They reflect humility; they show concern; they show sensitivity towards the other person's feelings by seeking forgiveness in asking a sensitive question. If you apologize in advance, in case you have inadvertently hurt someone's feeling, it shows a caring attitude.

Caution: If you apologize out of humility as a concerned human being then you are doing the right thing for the right reason. You don't need to apologize to be a good sales professional. Humility does not mean being over-apologetic either.

Keep your tone courteous and not commanding or demanding. Some people start telling a full history about the product without even asking any questions. The most important questions that a salesperson needs to think about are:

- How can you qualify a prospect without asking a question?
- How do you identify their need?
- How do you identify their hot buttons or buying motives?
- Would you like to go to a doctor, who, the moment you walked in, prescribed your medicine? Would you consider

him a good professional? He prescribes without asking about your problem. What do you call this practice? It is called malpractice. Similarly, what is the salesperson doing is he starts selling without finding out the need or the problem of the potential customer?

The important thing is to use questions to do some fact-finding. For example:

* How many employees do you have?
* What would be the color of the uniforms?
* How many would you need in each size – small, medium, large?

Questions to Understand More about the Prospect's Needs and Wants:

* What would you prefer? (Gets information)
* What are your thoughts about the new car? (Identifies opinion)
* What do you think about it? (Gives opinion)
* How comfortable are you with/do you feel about this? (Gives feeling)
* Is this what you mean . . . ? (Gives clarification or confirmation)
* Is it important? How crucial is this? (Gets information)

Questions pertaining to thinking and feeling are equally important, as answers to them reveal to you the prospect's level of interest.

While fact-finding, a good professional looks to identify the benefit that would help the prospect. A good professional must understand clearly what drives a prospect's decision and action. Typically, when a customer walks into a showroom, what do most sales people say?

'Can I help you?' and the customer says, *'No, I am just looking around.'* The conversation comes to an end. The salesperson just destroyed the sale. A company spends thousands of dollars, advertising, to get traffic coming into their store, but by having unprofessional or untrained sales people, potential clients are being chased out.

How would a good, professionally trained person approach a walk-in customer?

Imagine a scenario – A salesperson is at a furniture shop and a customer walks in. This is the way to approach him. After giving him 30 seconds to 1 minute, reasonable time to settle down and look around, the salesperson approaches him – (Caution: If the waiting period is too long a person may feel neglected. What is reasonable comes with experience. You don't want somebody jumping at your throat the moment you walk in.)

Salesperson: *'Good Morning'* or *'Welcome, how may I help you today?'*

1. Analyze this sentence as a greeting – is the tone warm, cold or fast? Is it dragging or too slow? Is the body language confident, upright or limp? If the salesman is sitting and he gets up in a reluctant manner, the customer feels guilty about disturbing the salesperson.

All of these will determine the attitude of the salesperson and eventually, the final outcome.

2. The actual words 'Good Morning' or 'Welcome' make a person feel wanted. People want to do business where they are wanted and welcomed. A potential customer gets a feeling that the salesperson also wants to do business with him or he needs and wants his business.

3. 'How may I help you?' – This cannot be answered in a 'yes' or 'no'. The prospect must give an answer.

4. It's good to include the word 'today' because we would like to close some business today.

Prospect: *'I'm just looking around',* or *'No thanks, I am just looking around.'*

Salesperson: *'I'm glad that you are, we have a large variety of furniture. What kind of furniture are you looking for?'*

Analysis

1. 'I am glad that you are' – is a reinforcing statement.

2. 'We have a large variety of furniture' – is a positive statement that we are well prepared and equipped to serve you.

3. 'What kind of furniture are you looking for?' – That's a probing question, which he cannot answer in a 'yes' or 'no' way.

Prospect: *'I am not sure, probably contemporary furniture?'*

Salesperson: *'Oh, that's great! Contemporary furniture looks*

> *wonderful in many homes. Which room were*
> *you looking for?'*

Analysis of the salesperson's approach:

1. 'Oh, that's great!' – is also a reinforcing/validation statement.
2. 'Contemporary furniture looks wonderful in many homes' – is a compliment.
3. 'Which room were you looking for?' – is a probing question that cannot be answered as either 'yes' or 'no'.

Prospect: *'The living room.'*
Salesperson: *'The living room happens to be the showcase of every home and we take pride in it, don't we?'*

Analysis:

'The living room happens to be the showcase of every home.' – Can he deny this statement? The most obvious answer is 'yes'. The salesperson has got an agreement, an acceptance and maybe a buy in.

The more 'yeses' the salesperson gets from the prospect, at every step of the presentation, the more difficult it will be for the prospect to say 'no' when the salesperson asks him for the order or the close.

Salesperson: *'In order to show you the right kind of furniture could I have the size of your living room?'*

Analysis:

'In order to show you the right kind of furniture' – the salesperson has given a reason to ask a question. Asking a question without giving a reason or making a positive statement might become interrogative and possibly offensive.

If you analyze the conversation so far, what is the salesperson doing? He is qualifying the prospect, which means till the prospect gets qualified, he is a suspect not a prospect. This is the responsibility of the sales professional. When a salesperson finds out that the customer is not a genuine buyer, the unprofessional salesperson would ignore the person and/or make them feel unwelcome, thus losing goodwill for themselves and their organization.

A good professional also values his time and doesn't want to waste the prospect's time either, but he does not ignore or leave the person or make him feel small, because to him, his and his organization's credibility is more important than the time spent in transitioning out with courtesy. A good professional understands that the cardinal rule of service is that, when a customer walks into your store, they have earned the right to courtesy, whether they purchase or not.

Analyze the entire conversation between the salesperson and the prospect. Before asking every question the salesperson made a positive statement in order to ensure that the questioning does not become interrogative or offensive.

Suppose he had not made a positive statement before asking a question, the conversation would have gone in the following manner. Imagine a scenario – a customer walks into a furniture store:

Salesperson:	*'How may I help you today?'*
Prospect:	*'I'm just looking around.'*
Salesperson:	*'What kind of furniture are you looking for?'*
Prospect:	*'I am not sure, probably contemporary furniture?'*
Salesperson:	*'Which room were you looking for?'*
Prospect:	*'The living room.'*
Salesperson:	*'What is the size of your living room?'*

If you notice in the above scenario the salesperson has just been asking questions one after the other, without making any positive statement, hence it becomes interrogative. Of course, the tone is important.

Many times you may have noticed that, at a social get-together, you meet someone for the first time and they start asking questions in a manner which becomes offensive. They meet you for the first time in your life and they ask:

- What's your name?
- Where do you live?
- What kind of work do you do?
- What's your turnover?
- What's your income?

As a listener, what's the first thing that comes to mind? 'Who are you and why don't you mind your own business?' What makes this offensive is that you feel as if you are being interrogated.

Supposing the conversation went in the following manner, it would be far more polite, courteous and open without being offensive. For example:

1. *My name is Shiv Khera, what's yours?*   He says: *I am so and so.*

2. *I live in New Jersey, where do you live?*   *I live in New York.*

3. *I am a consultant, what do you do for a living?*   *I am an engineer.*

If you notice, in all these 3 questions, before asking, I made a disclosure statement. Did I give any confidential information? Was there anything secret? No. My disclosure before the question showed openness and transparency. The other person does not feel threatened as to why he is being asked questions and willingly offers information.

In conclusion, questioning is a tool and if properly used can be a great asset. If not, it can give a lot of heartache. Hence, some important rules for questioning are:

1. Tone – keep it pleasant, polite, and courteous. Too soft might show timidity. Too loud might show aggressiveness or rudeness. A positive thing said in a negative manner has a negative meaning. A positive thing should be said in a positive manner.
2. Body language should be positive.
3. Make it a two-way conversation rather than a Q&A session.
4. As a matter of policy, the salesperson should take permission before asking questions by using these words, 'In order to suggest to you the right solutions do you mind if I ask you a few questions?'

The person who knows how to question tactfully, always leads and directs the conversation and is in control, besides gathering information and establishing credibility. When a prospect asks, '*What is the comparative advantage of buying your product over others?*'

A good professional would say something to the effect (in order to bring up the advantage), '*May I ask how familiar you are with our product?*' In most cases, chances are that the prospect may not be familiar with the product. In a situation like this, how can you even start answering the question unless you ask a question? Every question should lead us to the next base or step in the process of selling. If it does not, re-evaluate your question, you may need to change it. In case the sales professional is not clear about something, rather than saying, '*I am unclear or confused*', one can say – '*Just to clarify my thinking, could you please elaborate.................*'

The Power of Silence

Whenever you ask a question, wait for an answer. Some people become nervous when there is a silence. Their lack of confidence makes silence uncomfortable. That nervousness makes them break the silence and they jump in and break the pressure on the prospect. Silence can be a very effective way of communication; especially after asking a good question – it puts tremendous pressure on the prospect to reply.

Power of Listening

After you ask a question, it is crucial to listen actively and very carefully, both to what is being said and what is not being said. We need to observe the verbal and non-verbal communication. We need to listen and observe both words and feelings.

Listening gives clues to the salesperson to steer his presentation in the right direction. Listening identifies needs and wants and also identifies hot buttons. It also gives clues to objections for the skillful professional; there are tremendous advantages to help them close the sale.

Don't Sell, but Help the Customer to Buy

I had heard a sales trainer narrate the following story, which was possibly a scene on a television talk show.

> Someone asked a sales trainer, *'If you are so good in selling and you have trained so many people, then why don't you sell something to me right now?'*
>
> The sales trainer asked, *'What would you really like to buy?'*
>
> There was a pen lying on the table, so the man said, *'Sell me this pen.'*
>
> The trainer asked, *'Why would you want to have that pen?'*
>
> The man said, *'How can I function without a pen and besides, this one writes nicely too.'*
>
> The trainer then asked, *'Why else would you like to have this pen?'*
>
> The man replied, *'It is branded, it will give me prestige, aesthetically it looks nice and these are good enough reasons.'*
>
> The trainer asked, *'What do you think this pen is worth?'*
>
> The man said, *'I would say somewhere about $35. It's worth about $35.'*

The sales trainer said, '*Well, in that case I will let you own it for $35!*'

Just analyze the above transaction. Who sold what to whom? In fact, the buyer really bought the product, but the sales professional was in control because he directed the entire conversation by asking the right questions. This is a great example of good professional selling. In other words, the buyer sold himself.

19

LISTENING IS CARING

In communication, there are 2 elements involved: giving information and receiving information. Both are important, but listening is a little more important because it shows caring and it makes the other person feel significant, which in turn makes them more receptive to your ideas. Does it motivate them? The answer is YES.

Selling is asking pertinent questions, fact-finding, getting information, LISTENING VERY CAREFULLY and then offering solutions. 90% of the solution lies in properly identifying the problem. Selling is about problem-solving. Problems can only be uncovered and accurately identified if one listens carefully.

Listening versus Hearing

There is a difference between listening and hearing. Listening is active, hearing is passive. Listening is emotional, hearing is physical. Active listening takes this a step further and goes beyond just the spoken words to looking for hidden messages and recognizing feelings.

Creating a Positive Environment

1) While listening, avoid creating distractions such as playing with a pen or the paper-weight or tapping your fingers. It creates competition for your mind.

2) Most people do not communicate, they simply take turns talking. While one is speaking, what is the listener doing in reality? He is thinking of what he has to say next. When the speaker becomes the listener, he does the same thing. Both are speaking, nobody is listening. So, slow down, listen to the prospect, and collect your thoughts before responding. The more prepared you are, the better you will be at responding. Remember, two monologues do not make a dialogue.

3) Don't interrupt. It is bad manners and even if you think you know what the other person is about to say, you might be making a wrong assumption.

4) Acknowledge and encourage the other person by nodding your head, smiling and occasionally saying 'yes' or something to that effect. Recognize and acknowledge others' feelings.

5) Maintain eye contact, without staring at the other person. Don't keep looking around the room or outside as that makes the other person wary.

6) A warm smile shows interest.

7) Ask questions to clarify and make notes.

8) Rephrase and paraphrase to show that you understand.

9) Don't finish the other person's sentence. Show respect.

10) Keep the conversation focussed and to the point.

11) Don't behave as if you know it all.

12) Don't act as if by listening you are doing them a favor.

Evaluate the Communication

Take a short time-out in the middle of a discussion to reflect on how things are progressing. Sometimes, the subconscious mind needs a little time to process information to think of new ideas. You can excuse yourself politely and speak to a colleague. This needs to be done very carefully to ensure that it doesn't offend the prospect. One can say something like, 'With your permission can I just take a break for 2 minutes to get fresh air?' Analyze the above scenario. Do you have to give reasons for wanting to get some fresh air? The answer is no. The tone and the words used with the non-verbal body language put together would determine your politeness. By the way, this is not uncommon, especially at the time of major negotiations. This little break would give you time to ask yourself the following questions: Are you doing most of the talking? Have you understood what the customer wants?

Are you being cool, calm and collected? What can you tell from the non-verbal language?

Active listening will give you clues and help you identify buying motives. For example, an unsure body language generally brings out a verbal objection. Generally sitting or standing cross-armed represents that the person is either holding back or resisting in some manner. A positive body language is a signal of encouragement.

How do you encourage a prospect to speak and to share more information? A good salesperson should speak less and listen more. He should listen very attentively and actively to what is said and what is unsaid by analyzing both the verbal and non-verbal. A prospect will only speak if he feels comfortable and is encouraged by the salesperson through his questioning technique and his positive intervention, or remarks such as:

1. 'That sounds very interesting.'
2. 'Can you elaborate a little more?'
3. 'Great timing!'
4. 'Quick, sharp thinking!'

The salesperson should be smiling and nodding as this shows acknowledgement and encourages the other person to speak. Another way to get the prospect to talk is to rephrase or paraphrase the feedback. While doing this, the salesperson should use some key words mentioned by the prospect, as it shows connection. It also reconfirms that your interpretation is in line with his thinking. This is how the salesperson should bring it up:

1. 'Mr Prospect, just to clarify my thinking, does this reflect what you meant . . . ?'
2. 'Mr Prospect, just to reconfirm . . . '

Barriers to Effective Communication

There are 3 broad categories of barriers – physical, emotional and intellectual.

Physical – Barriers are such as noise distraction, doodling, drumming with fingers or playing with a pen/paperweight, a non-conducive environment, constant disturbance or not maintaining eye-contact. Do you have the appropriate distance between you and the prospect to create warmth and avoid discomfort? Physical barriers could also include ill health, tiredness, etc.

Emotional – Emotions are somehow connected without saying anything. Have you been to a social event where you noticed several people enjoying, laughing and having fun till one person walks in and there is a pin-drop silence. The reverse is also true, everybody is a guest in the room and one person walks in and brightens the place. So, in a discussion, seek to build empathy and trust by observing your verbal and non-verbal communications and show the prospect that you have a connection and that you believe that he is important and respected.

Intellectual – What you say, I will evaluate, and what I say, you will evaluate, and based on this interpretation, we accept or reject. Example of a bad presentation is intellectual comprehension at different levels. Use everyday spoken language that buyers understand and seek to build rapport and influence through layering of positive actions and agreements. As you achieve this, the prospect will increasingly feel that you are a credible speaker.

Ego Barrier – Have you ever been in a conversation where no matter what you say, the other person either contradicts you or elaborates on what you said? No matter what you say, they are permanently on the other side, or they have something better to add. The spirit of communication seems to be argumentative. It seems they have an instinctive compulsion to be on the opposite side.

For example: If you say, *'I think it is too hot today.'*
The other person will say, *'I don't think so. I think it is pleasant today.'*
And if you said the reverse, *'I think it is pleasant today,'* you can predict the response of the other person.
He would say, *'I think it is hot/cold today.'* Are these contradictions just coincidental? I don't think so. I think it is habitual and part of a person's personality.

The process of selling needs openness and coming together on sharing needs, thoughts and feelings. Disagreements increase the risk of losing the sale. This means that agreements increase the probability of sales. In fact, every agreement results in both sides feeling good. Disagreements put people on a defensive or confrontational position and many times the transparency disappears. Disagreements or argumentative behavior also reflect that you have a need to show that you are in control. Perhaps, it is a need to satisfy a deprived ego.

One-upmanship comes out of insecurity or low self-esteem. The need to show yourself as superior also comes for the same reason. It is something you see not only in schools or colleges but in offices also – the attitude that 'mine is better than yours' or that 'I am better than you'. This is a common phenomenon in social life too. This behavior, instead of bringing people closer, pushes them apart. A person who is insecure feels superior when he makes the other person feel inferior. They belittle or reduce the importance of another person's contribution to one of insignificance. People who are secure, appreciate and build other people's self-esteem. These are the people who listen well and then respond appropriately.

Discourteous and ill-mannered behavior can also manifest as a big barrier to effective communication. Example 1) Constant interruptions. 2) Not letting the other person complete a sentence. 3) Finishing the sentence of the other person.

Bad Timing

Before making a presentation, always check the receptivity of the other person. Do not start your presentation when the prospect is pre-occupied. There are times when a prospect is pre-occupied with many other things and is unable to concentrate while listening to a presentation. It is much better not to make a presentation at that time. The better thing is to reschedule the appointment or break the pre-occupation without offending the other person.

Pre-occupation could also be because of impatience. Your client is running late for an appointment or has to catch a flight. Would it be advisable to make a presentation at that time? Do you think he would be listening to you? The answer, obviously, is no.

Unfortunately, many sales people do not recognize or realize that they are imposing themselves on the other person.

The cardinal rule is never to make a presentation till you have the prospect's undivided attention. Why? If he is not listening to you and you make the entire presentation, he may keep nodding and you think he is agreeing with you but he is not even interested and you are wasting your time. If you do this, do you think you would end up closing the sale? The answer is no.

Don't Let Your Tongue Cut Your Throat by Speaking Too Much

Some people are good talkers – their talking ability helps them make a sale. But they don't know when to stop. They talk too much. In fact, they talk themselves out of the sale. Their (talking ability) strength got them in. When over-extended, it became a weakness. Giving too much information right at the beginning of the presentation can confuse the prospect and lead to a lost opportunity. Communication should be clear, concise and done with confidence. A casual sentence to start a conversation or the process of building rapport should not end up in a socializing session:

- Remember the actual purpose of the visit
- You are wasting your time and that of the prospect
- Your prospect could get irritated or he may find you entertaining and pleasant but unprofessional

The ability to think and make good judgments is crucial, which means we need to know and trust ourselves to be able to say the right thing, at the right time and in the right manner. Developing instincts and good judgment comes from experience. Your strengths can get you into a sales discussion, but don't get over-extended and let your own strengths become a liability.

How Much Information Should You Give to Your Prospect?

Do you want to make your prospect an expert in your product? The answer is: No, of course not. You have put a lot of time and effort in learning your trade. You are not looking to transfer all your knowledge to your client. Why should you?

A sales professional's job is to educate the prospect only enough to help him make an intelligent decision. Giving too much information is another barrier in sales. Keep in mind that making a presentation is like performing on the stage. You are looking for a standing ovation, which is the measure of the quality of your performance. In a sales scenario, the measure of your performance is the decision to purchase.

It is the obligation of a salesperson to make sure that the prospect's time is well utilized. The prospect has done you a favor by granting you his valuable time. It is, therefore, your obligation to make sense.

Taking Notes

I would like to elaborate on why taking notes in writing is important. It shows seriousness and that you are not just relying on memory alone. The non-caring person hears 8 or 10 points and thinks he will recall all of them and do the job. It is only human that once in a while we may remember most and forget a few. Hence what have we done? An incomplete job. Just analyze the above. Does this happen? Do people behave like this? The answer is yes. What kind of attitude does it show? In my opinion, an unprofessional and non-caring attitude. A caring person would ensure to take written notes very carefully in great detail. Before leaving, he would reconfirm that he has not missed out anything. That shows professionalism. To me, dealing with people who do not take detailed and careful notes always gives discomfort and raises doubts on their intent, and in their ability and willingness to deliver.

You must be in-charge. You must control the entire interview!

20

POSITIVE COMMUNICATION
FOR SELLING

Communication

The big barrier in selling is the communication barrier. The biggest communication barrier is the difference in perception of the buyer and the salesperson. If the salesperson has good persuasion skills then he can make the buyer perceive things his way. Persuasion is defined as the ability to influence or change a person's belief system.

In order to do his job with integrity and authenticity, a good salesperson needs to be very clear about:

1. His values – what he would or would not do
2. Commitment to the customers

3. Product knowledge
4. Policies and procedures

A lack of knowledge and commitment can result in miscommunication. We communicate all the time either through words, silence or through actions.

Non-verbal Communication

A professional must become aware of both verbal and non-verbal communication. Dr Albert Mehrabian did a study and came to the conclusion that 55% of our communication is non-verbal, 38% related to the tone and only 7% is verbal. Guess which one we give the most importance to – verbal.

The salesperson should listen to words, feelings and thought patterns. Observe if there is congruence or mismatch in the verbal and non-verbal behavior. Whenever there is a contradiction between verbal and non-verbal, which one should we believe? The answer is 'non-verbal,' because the non-verbal is a reflex action arising from the subconscious. The communicator is not aware that it's happening. For instance, the communicator may be saying, 'I'm very interested in what you are saying,' but at the same time is looking at his watch or the ceiling fan or doing something else. Is he really interested? Does the non-verbal show interest and attentiveness in this case? Certainly not.

Openness and acceptance can be communicated through positive body language. Resistance and rejection can also be communicated with disagreeable body language. Non-verbal communication comprises posture, gestures, hand movements, eye contact and facial expressions.

Some common examples of body language to look out for:

1. A prospect sitting with crossed arms or crossed legs shows lack of openness.
2. Leaning forward shows interest.
3. Facial expressions can also reveal buying or rejection signals.

Our non-verbal behavior or body language is driven by our subconscious which reveals our thought process. For example:

1. Eye contact –
   a. Staring directly at your prospect could be taken as a sign of arrogance, aggression or rude. Having shifty eyes can communicate uneasiness, sliminess or cunningness. Gazing at the ceiling or the fan shows a lack of interest or a non-caring attitude.
   b. Comfortable eye contact establishes trust, builds confidence and reflects sincerity.
2. Posture – Don't slouch or lean back. This can be interpreted as a lack of attentiveness or disinterest.
3. Body movements – Jerky movements show edginess and nervousness or even a lack of confidence.
4. Gestures – Yawning, playing with a pen or doodling, all indicate indifference.
5. Facial expressions – Stiff or uptight expressions or smiling sarcastically gives a negative impression.
6. Overall grooming – Professional appearance. You find professionals wear clothes that are not too trendy. They dress conservatively. A financial planner or banker

would generally come in a formal suit or if it is too hot for the jacket, he would come in formal trousers, shirt and tie. He would not be dressed in jeans and sports shoes.

Be observant about body language. It will save you time and increase your chances of closing a sale.

Verbal

When dealing with another person, one's tone should be pleasant and the pace of speech should be moderate – not too fast and not too slow.

Good sales professionals use words that are specific in order to ensure transferring the same picture into the prospect's mind, resulting in clarity of communication or bringing up the same perception to the giver and the receiver. Hence abstain from using vague words that have multiple meanings such as:

- Almost always
- Occasionally
- Regularly
- Frequently
- Sometimes, and
- Seldom

All these words are non-committal, unspecific and raise doubt. They create suspicion and hesitation in the mind of the buyer. Be careful of how you phrase your sentences, for example:

1. 'My investment is lower,' or 'You could probably save more.'

Both these statements are non-specific. We need to clarify how much lower and how much saving exists.

2. 'This polish can help you clean your home faster,' or 'This polish could save you time and allow you to use your time more productively.'
   How much faster?

All these words are confusing and end up creating doubt in the buyer's mind because the same words mean different things to different people, which becomes an obstacle in closing a sale.

Clarify vague statements that could have multiple meanings. For example: It costs too much. This could mean many things, such as:

1. I don't have that much money.
2. This is not worth the price.
3. It is more expensive as compared to your competitors.

This one statement could mean anything. In order to be able to answer effectively, the salesperson needs to clarify by asking questions tactfully or through carefully worded statements. For example:

1. 'Is this your major concern?'
2. 'What are your other concerns?'
3. 'You just mentioned . . . but somehow I get a feeling you seem to be a little uncomfortable with . . . could I request you to share your thoughts with me . . . ?'

What are Buying Signals?

Buying signals can be both verbal and/or non-verbal. Recognizing buying signals is crucial to closing a sale. At times, there are opportunities to get a commitment for sale. Be sensitive to the clues. When you recognize the buying signals, that's the time you may want to cut down your presentation and go for the close. Make the transition carefully and don't be abrupt. A good way of transitioning is to summarize the benefits (not more than 3 benefits at a time). Then start the paperwork.

Verbal Buying Signals:

The prospect starts asking you questions such as:

- Can I pay for this monthly?
- Can this vacuum cleaner clean the curtains also?
- How much will it cost?
- When can I have the delivery?
- Can I have it delivered on Saturday morning?
- What kind of warranty/guarantee do you have?
- Do you have any annual maintenance contract?
- Can you show it to me again?
- Can you demonstrate it one more time?
- What kind of credit facilities do you give?
- Do you have any instalment plans?
- How many colors does it come in?
- Can I try it one more time?

Positive buying signals are like green lights for you to go ahead, and the opposite is just as true. Negative buying signals are your stop signs, which mean the prospect is telling you, 'I am not convinced yet.'

What are Rejection Signals?

Many times the prospect may not want to say 'no' directly, hence they may find alternate ways to express the rejection in a polite manner. Some rejections may be for genuine reasons. For instance, if he is genuinely over-stocked, then it stands to reason that he has no space to put the merchandise even if you give it for free. 'I want to think it over' is often a polite way of saying, 'I am not interested.'

Verbal Rejection Signals

1. This doesn't seem to be more reliable than my current system.
2. Can you leave the information and I will call you later?
3. I don't have any warehousing capacity for this merchandize.
4. I am sure your price will be the same a year from now.
5. I want to think it over.

A sudden change in behavior or body language may reflect a change in attitude – a **non-verbal rejection**. Whenever a good sales professional sees or hears rejection signals he realizes that there is a lack of interest from the prospect and he needs to take a decision either to resell, reschedule or remove himself from in front of the prospect. One needs to be sensitive to both verbal and non-verbal signs. Upon observing rejection signals, a salesperson could say something to the effect:

1. 'Mr Prospect, it seems that something is disturbing you. Could I request you to share it with me?'
2. 'Inadvertently, if I have made any mistake, I seek forgiveness.'
3. 'I apologize, but could you share your concerns?'

A good sales professional is like the driver of a car. He sees the traffic signal and understands that when it is a red light, it's time to stop. When it is green, it's time to go. A sharp salesperson needs to recognize buying signals when they are red, yellow or green.

Don't Use Jargon

Use layman's language or commonly used technical language. When you go to buy a computer, notice how often you'll walk away from a shop after a salesperson has downloaded you with a lot of technical information, and you're left thinking that you don't really know what you want. A salesperson may ask how many megabytes or gigabytes you want in a storage device. Only a tech-savvy consumer can understand this. For the prospect, he may not understand this, but his only need is to know if it can store 2,000 A4 size pages. Don't use jargon unless you are speaking to someone in your own profession.

Words that create objections or resistance

Prevent objections by choosing your words carefully:

1. Replace words like 'buy/sell' with 'own.' For example, 'After you own this product . . .' Nobody likes to be sold something as it implies a lack of control. Ownership gives stability and pride.

2. Don't use the word 'sign'. Replace it with, 'Can you confirm this order?'

3. Avoid the word 'contract'. People are afraid of this word as they do not know what they are getting into. They feel as if they'll need to bring a lawyer into the discussions. Replace it with, 'Let's get the formalities/paperwork/agreement out of the way.'

4. Do not use words like 'price/payment/money/pay/cash/cost.' Replace them with the word 'investment'. For example, rather than saying 'after you pay' or 'your cost will be so much,' you can say 'your one time/monthly investment would be X'. Why? This is because words like price, payment and cost imply a loss – an out-of-pocket, 'gone forever' feeling. On the other hand, 'investment' implies that the person is getting something back in return and the truth is they are. Everybody wants to be an investor. There is pride to be an investor. Who wants to be a payer?

5. The one phrase which I use regularly and which I have found to bring about positive feelings and progress in a discussion is 'Let me share with you some information that has been helpful to many people such as yourself.' Isn't this better than simply saying, 'Let me tell you about

my product'?

Do not use phrases and questions that are harmful, such as:

+ I will try to/I hope to
+ Maybe/It should be
+ Perhaps/Probably
+ That could happen/It sounds right
+ We can't
+ Only important or major clients are entitled
+ You don't qualify
+ That's not my department
+ I don't handle that
+ That's not my responsibility
+ Do you understand?
+ Let me tell you
+ When will you decide?
+ When will you make up your mind?
+ What's your problem?
+ If you don't decide, you will miss out all
+ Shouldn't you be doing
+ I think so

All these words can have a negative effect. On the other hand, positive words are encouraging, supportive and demonstrate care and graciousness. Here are a few words that I have found to be powerful and have helped open doors for me. Even though they're common words, they convey a positive message and help in selling.

Advantage	Amazing	Comprehensive	Competitive edge	Critical
Impactful	Crucial	Enhanced	Extraordinary	Eye-catching
Evident	Improved	Measurable	Profitable	Proven
Personal	Respected	Safe	Significant	Special
Timely	Tested	Thorough	Tremendous	Verified
Productive	Effective	Important	Dynamic	Grow

Phrases and questions that are helpful:

- How do you feel about . . . ?
- What do you think about? How about considering this?
- Let's face it . . .
- Together I am sure we can . . .
- Were you aware of?
- May I ask for your help?
- I am sure you would not want to gamble with . . .
- Could I request you to clarify . . .
- What's your opinion about . . . ?
- I suggest . . . or may I suggest . . . ?
- In my opinion . . .
- What do you feel is the best way?
- We're sure that we can . . .
- What is your first priority?
- Would you be comfortable with . . .

21

UNCOVERING THE NEED

There are 2 Kinds of Needs – Visible and Invisible

The **visible** need is where the prospect is aware of the pain or the problem and actively responds to or takes action, without somebody prompting him. They have a sense of urgency and are proactive in their buying activity. These needs are like food, clothing and shelter. They are necessities. People go out and purchase them. Price may not be a consideration.

The **invisible** need is where the prospect has to be made aware of the gain in owning and the pain of not having. When we talk of the profession of selling, we refer to the market segment of the invisible need. This represents the majority of the market segment and an opportunity for the selling profession.

I estimate that the market share of visible needs runs in single digits but for the invisible needs it's infinite. In my career of selling life insurance, I don't think I have ever got a call from any prospect saying, 'Please come and sell me life insurance because I need it.' That means almost 100% of the output comes from invisible needs. What could possibly be the cause for invisible needs? Why don't people recognize the needs that do exist?

- **Complacence** – People resist change; if it is not broken, don't fix it. They wait for something to break and then their need turns from invisible to visible. That's the person who waits for a disaster or an emergency and then develops the urgency to manage it.
- **Indifference** – The 'who cares,' 'it's not my job,' 'no feeling of belonging,' 'I only work here,' 'everybody knows of the problem' attitude. If everyone knows the problem, then how can I be accountable? This is a non-caring attitude.
- **Ignorance** – The prospect does not know that he does not know. He needs to be educated.

The moment a good sales professional can address any of these issues, he brings urgency into the buyer's mind to buy now and not later. This explains how to handle a buyer's specific objection: 'What's the urgency? I will do it later.' The process of education or providing relevant information helps transform the invisible need into a visible one. It changes the buyer's behavior from being reactive to proactive. A prospect cannot take advantage of a solution of which he is not aware. A good sales professional brings to surface the loss from waiting. Sales people who are looking for visible needs invariably fail in the profession.

For example, a water-purifier salesperson, John, is literally going out of business, whereas his competitor Steve has so much business that he cannot handle it. This is because John's approach was to look for people with visible needs and his opening presentation was something like, '*I am with XYZ Company and we sell water filters,*' but Steve's approach was totally different and as follows:

Steve: '*Mr Prospect, my name is Steve. I am with XYZ Water Filter Company. Are you aware that the number of people falling sick because of water-borne diseases in your area has doubled in the last 1 year?*'

Prospect: '*Really? I didn't know about it.*'

Steve: '*Unfortunately, in the last 30 days, there have been close to 10 cases in your neighborhood. I am here to provide information as to how you could protect your family from such water-borne diseases. May I come in?*'

Prospect: '*Of course.*'

Steve: '*Mr Prospect, for the next 30 days we are offering a complimentary water analysis report to those who are concerned for the well-being of their family, without any obligation to buy anything. We shall send our technician to take a sample of your water supply, give you a detailed report, identify areas of risks, if any, and give suggestions on how to rectify them.*'

Based on the above conversation, Steve was able to set up appointments one after the other for complimentary analysis and with every suggestion for eliminating health hazards and risk from water-borne diseases, Steve got an opportunity to identify an invisible need. With every presentation that Steve made, he could point out to the prospect, the diseases that could cause trouble to the family.

Hence, he created an urgency to remedy the situation and the buyer invariably ended up asking, *'How soon can you correct the situation and how much will it cost?'*

Analyze the difference between Steve and John's approach. Steve was able to successfully uncover the need, show the urgency (cost of waiting or potential pain from waiting), provide the solution and close the sale. It was a win-win situation. Whereas John was not really selling, he was waiting for somebody to buy from him. In other words, he really is not in the profession of selling. He is an order taker. Steve always looked at himself as someone providing a valuable service to society. If you notice carefully, a good professional like Steve never created a problem. Steve did not use any fear tactic nor did he create urgency. He did not create a need for water filters. It was already there. He just uncovered it and made the prospect aware of both the need and urgency to act, which enabled the buyer to take an educated decision. If you further analyze Steve's approach, he was not selling water filters but providing good health, stress-free living and a better quality of life. The same principle applies for all products, no matter what we sell.

While selling life insurance, very often I was asked, 'Why do I need any life insurance? I am not dying anytime soon.

I am in good health and I don't need life insurance.' What they did not realize is that if they are not in good health, they will not get any life insurance as then they do not qualify to get a policy. They had to be made aware that life insurance was like a life jacket. If they didn't have it, they would never realize they need it.

Sometimes, we are told, 'Our revenues are down, hence we don't need any sales training.' They don't realize the invisible need. If their sales people were skillful, their sales would go up. These are clear examples of uncovering invisible needs. The example of the vacuum cleaner salesman given earlier in this book is a clear example of a salesman uncovering an invisible need.

22

FEATURES AND BENEFITS

❦

People don't buy features, they buy benefits. People don't buy movie tickets, they buy entertainment. People don't buy neckties, they buy good looks. People don't buy perfumes, they buy sweet smells.

Michael Faraday invented the electrical motor. He did not have the money to market it commercially. He was looking for funds rather desperately. He approached the UK Prime Minister, Mr Gladstone, and placed his invention on his table, expecting a great response. The prime minister, however, could not see any use or benefit in his invention and said something to the effect: *'What good is it, and I don't see how we can use this motor?'* Today, can you imagine this world without an electrical motor? One can hardly find a place where it isn't used.

Faraday could have been very disappointed and have said to himself or the prime minister, *'How can you not see the potential use of this invention? Look at the hard work that I have put in.'*

However, he didn't do that. His response was to show the benefit and he said to the prime minister, *'Someday, you might be able to raise money through taxes by the sale of this machine.'* What did he do? He immediately showed the benefit to the prime minister and appealed to his buying motive. To the politician, the buying motive was to raise funds for the government.

Turning a Feature into a Benefit – 'What it means to you is . . .'

The biggest mistake that most sales people make is that they take their product and a bag full of literature, overwhelm the prospect and start talking about the features. Whether the product is made from this material or another one, whether it is made in one country or another, who cares! These people are peddling, not selling. A professional knows how to sell a benefit or how to convert a feature into a benefit.

This phrase is very important: 'What it means to you is . . .'

A feature is stated and what it means to the prospect is mentioned in the form of benefits.

For example:

1. The car's tyre size is X or this car is equipped with power brakes and ABS. 'What it means to you is that when you

are driving on the highway it will give you tremendous safety.' Here, the salesperson is giving the benefit of safety.

2. When he talks of upholstery or heavy-duty shock absorbers, he says, 'What it means to you is a comfortable drive and when you get out from the car, you will feel fresh.'

3. Untrained computer sales people sell the technicalities which people often don't understand. More sales would have taken place if they just told the potential customer how the additional speed translates into a saving for him. 'The 30% faster speed means 20% saving, which means an additional profit of 5%, a result of greater output for the same cost.'

4. A good sales professional selling trousers asks a customer, 'Do you travel quite a bit? If so, this trouser is wrinkle-free. What this means to you is that even after a whole day of travel, it will remain uncreased and it will appear as if you are wearing a fresh trouser.'

5. Stock brokers/real estate agents help people make money. (At least, so they claim.)

6. Insurance agents provide savings and security.

7. A faster new photocopier saves time, increases productivity/profitability and cuts cost.

8. Purchasing a Mercedes gives pleasure, prestige and peace of mind.

Feature	Gain Benefit/Avoid Pain
Strong/Strength	Cost saving
Durable	Safety/Security
Speed	Dependability/Reliability

Feature	Gain Benefit/Avoid Pain
Big	Saves time
Small	Make money
Good quality	Feel good
Accurate/Accuracy	Comfort/Convenience
Prompt delivery	Compact
Latest technology	Longer lasting
Online service	Peace of mind
Over the phone service	Prestige/recognition
Less power consumption	Status symbol
	Increase productivity
	Eliminate fear of loss
	Convenience
	Gives pleasure
	Gives health

Examples of features are: shape, size, color, delivery, benchmarks, standards, contents, specifications, packaging, etc. Features describe a product. They don't explain a benefit. Speed is a feature, time and money-saving are benefits. Customers always buy 'perceived values'. They never buy features or price.

A good sales professional will always tie the benefit to a specific need of the customer which is called 'personalization and value addition'. The resulting advantage/positive consequence of a feature becomes a benefit. A beautiful glass door is a feature. How do you translate it into a benefit? It gives an open look. The visibility attracts people, increases traffic, increases sales and profitability goes up.

In today's competitive world, most companies can match features but the biggest differentiating factor is the people behind the company, starting from the salesperson. This is why, before a customer buys a product, he buys the salesperson. The best company or product will be rejected if the salesperson does not build a level of comfort in the buyer. **First, the potential customer buys the salesperson, then the product and company.**

The benefits fall in 2 categories – either to gain a benefit or to avoid a loss. These 2 can be further divided into increased productivity, profitability, convenience, security, peace of mind, savings, status, etc. Just as the beauty lies in the eyes of the beholder, similarly, a benefit only becomes a benefit when the customer perceives it as such. Lead-free paint is a feature whereas good health or healthy living is a benefit.

Product/service	Gain	Avoid loss
Life Insurance	Gives peace of mind, security	Prevents disaster in case of untimely death
Multi-vitamins	Good health	Illness
Cosmetics	Good looks	Uncertainty as to how you look or smell

A Benefit Opener – Approach

By way of another example, consider this case: 'Mr Prospect, my name is XYZ. I am calling from . . . would you have a minute to talk? We sent you an invitation for a book launch – have you received it or do you remember seeing it?

Mr Prospect, we have received an overwhelming response. Since we have not received an RSVP from you and knowing that you would like to take advantage of this opportunity, I am calling to ensure that we hold a seat for you.'

Just analyze the above conversation. The sales professional brings out the benefit and that the prospect should not lose out on an opportunity. He did not ask or request the prospect to come and attend. In other words, what is he doing? Is he selling a benefit to provide a gain or avoid pain? At the same time, he made it easy for the prospect to make a commitment to attend the launch. However, he does not stop there. He ensures the prospect's attendance by saying, 'I shall hold a seat for you and would request that you kindly make a note in your calendar.' Then a good professional would go one step further – he would call up the prospect's secretary, inform her about the conversation and ask her to block that time in the calendar, and not only that, he would also send a fax or an e-mail.

Does this guarantee that the prospect will be there? The answer is no. Does it increase the probability of his being there – the answer is YES.

Remember:
ALWAYS SELL THE SIZZLE, NOT THE STEAK!

23

ABC OF SELLING

A BC stands for **ALWAYS BE CLOSING**. It is a good philosophy to practice, provided you have earned the right to close. What gives you the right to close? Ask yourself, if you have established rapport and gotten mutual agreement and acceptance on needs and solutions. Timing is crucial. Knowing when to close is like baking a dish. Taking it out too soon could leave the dish uncooked and baking it too long could burn it. In trying to close too soon or too late, you may lose out an opportunity that you may never get again. Recognizing the most appropriate timing to close is intuitive and comes from experience.

Sales Presentations

Whenever a prospect asks a question, a good professional will rephrase and repeat the question. This is because:

* It gives him time to think and fully understand the question.
* By rephrasing the question, he clarifies the real issue. By crystallizing and reconfirming, it shows that he actually understood the concern of the prospect.
* If the prospect's question does not carry substance and has some level of irrelevance, chances are the prospect would recognize it and probably withdraw the objection by saying, 'Forget it.'

If the prospect asks, '*How many colors does it come in?*' A good professional would say, '*It comes in 3 colors – red, blue and green and blue happens to be the most desired and popular one. Which would you prefer – the blue, the red or the green?*' Again, if you notice, it ends by the salesperson asking for the order.

As another example, the prospect asks what size/capacity the product comes in. Rather than just giving all the sizes, a good professional will always end the answer with a trial close. For instance, 'It comes in small, medium, large and extra large. The medium and large sizes account for 80% of our business, which one would you prefer the most?'

In case your prospect asks for something that you do not offer or sell (any allied products), one can always say, 'We do not carry that product as part of our business, but we have a business partner who does.' You notice that the ending is not negative or 'no'. Do not make a false promise. If you do not have an allied partner, do not lie. The right thing then would be to say, 'I am sorry, we do not carry that particular item, but here are some alternatives I can suggest.'

Sometimes, a restaurant may run out of something from the menu and if the customer asks for that particular item, a waiter does not say, 'Sorry, we ran out of this item,' and stop; rather, he says, 'I am sorry we have run out of this item, but I could offer you 2 other, very similar choices, which are our speciality. Which one would you prefer, this or the other?'

Evaluate the conversation – is the server telling the truth? The answer is yes. Should he have stopped after saying, 'No, we have run out of it'? The answer is no. By giving the customer an additional 2 choices, is he doing something wrong? Is he being dishonest, is he manipulating them or forcing them to buy? No. By not giving an additional choice to the customer is he doing his job right? No. Why? Is he not depriving himself and his organization of a potential sale? Yes. Similarly, does a salesperson have an obligation to (a) the customer to offer the opportunity to make a positive choice, and (b) his organization, by offering to sell in an honest manner by enhancing the company's sale ethically? Is he doing the right job for his company? Yes.

Once, our office received a phone call from a different town, from someone who wanted to purchase our books and DVDs. It was a little late in the evening and coincidentally we had a new employee attending to the call. This novice, without asking any questions said to the client, 'Why don't you go to the closest book store in your town and buy from there?'

Instead of finding out what difficulty the customer was facing and why he couldn't find the book, he asked if there was a book stall near him. Even if there was a book stall, was there a sense of emergency? Regardless, he could and should have taken the contact details and couriered the materials without delay, resulting in satisfaction for all sides. The customer would have been satisfied, the company would have made a sale and the salesperson would have done his job. It would have ended up being a profitable transaction for both the parties. Obviously, in the scenario above, either we, as a company, had not properly trained the person or if we had trained him properly and he still continued to do as above, then it showed that he had no sense of belonging to the company, and a bad attitude.

If the prospect asks a question that you don't have an answer to, a dishonest person tries to make up an answer to show how smart he is. A good professional on the other hand only says, 'I don't have the answer to this question, but if I have your permission I will call up my office and get an answer for you right now', or 'I will get back to you by tomorrow evening'. An honest person would also ensure that he does get back within the specified time. A good salesperson would not be vague, non-committal and say, 'I will get back to you as soon as possible or I will try to get the answer for you. I should be able to get it in a day or two, or you can call and check with me later.' Such statements raise doubts, and hence weaken the salesperson's and their organization's position and credibility.

In case of any objection, a good sales professional can handle most queries with the 'feel, felt, found' formula, by saying, 'I understand how you **feel** . . . some other people **felt** that way too, till they tried the machine and **found** that the increase in productivity far out-weighed the investment.' In asking, 'What would you prefer, red or blue?' If you notice, – the ending is with a trial close.

A good professional always looks for an opportunity to build the other person's self-esteem. One simple and easy way is to give sincere appreciation or a compliment to the prospect by saying something like, 'That's a very good question,' or 'Thank you for asking,' or 'I am glad you asked'. Secondly, the compliment must be sincere. Don't just give it because people can see through it and you will appear fake and untruthful.

Caution: Once you say that that's a good question, the next time he asks another question, if you don't say it is a good question, does it mean it is a bad question? Do you always say, 'That's a good question,' each time after the prospect asks a question? The answer is no. Be careful, be selective; use commonsense and be sincere.

Don't oversell yourself, your product or your company. If you are demonstrating a product, it is generally a good idea to always let the customer use as many sensory factors as you can – such as touch, taste, sight, feel, experience, smell. There is an old saying, 'The proof of the pudding is in the eating,' which stands true even today. That is why many people give samples for touching and tasting. When the prospect likes the sample then they want more of it. Be careful, give only enough to give a taste for evaluation purposes, not to satisfy hunger. It gives the prospect a level of comfort.

Always, make an effort to have your prospect sit next to you rather than opposite you. Generally, sitting opposite may subconsciously appear conflicting or confrontational, but sitting next to the prospect sends the message that we are both on the same team. It shows togetherness. Preferably, have the client sit to your right, though it is not crucial. This is why many executives have started having round tables in their offices, rather than sitting across each other.

Up-selling and Cross Selling

Typically, many people call up our office asking for information on the program, availability and price. Our sales executive finds out more about the customer's needs through skillful fact-finding, for which we have developed a questionnaire. After a person has enrolled into one program, they are asked questions to see if we can uncover an invisible need for the second program.

In order for professionals to maximize the revenue from a customer, they need to understand the following, and in particular, have this information on their fingertips and be able to articulate it clearly as they are nearing the completion of a sale:

- The relationship between different products that the company sells. If a customer typically has a need for one, what else might he be looking to buy at the same time or soon afterwards?
- Can the additional products be sold without hurting the first sale?
- Don't assume that the customer knows what's available to him. It's your job to help him raise his understanding. Imagine if the customer buys only 50% of what he could have bought, he may later think that you have

not done your job by not explaining what he was required to do, in order to complete the purchase.

Good professionals always need to think in terms of customer's needs and wants, but they also need to understand what they can offer and to articulate it in real time. One should ensure that the prospect is entirely comfortable with the first purchase before offering the second one. By extending the discussion onto other products, he might even lose the first purchase.

Cross Sell

This is where the sales professional seeks to sell a different, but related product to the customer, alongside the first one. For example, when training programs are held in 5 different locations, a good professional would sell multiple locations by cross selling. Another example is:

* 'You're really going to enjoy this bike, Mr Prospect. It'll enhance your experience if you own a set of front/rear lights and a safety helmet. For a small investment of $23, you would want them both, wouldn't you?

Up-selling

You go to a bank to open a current account. A good sales professional, after opening the current account, would offer the bank's other services such as safety deposit box, savings account, fixed deposit, etc. This is called up-selling.

Generally, the most appropriate time to cross sell or up-sell is immediately after you have made your first sale. This is because your credibility has been established and the additional advantage comes at a very low incremental outlay.

Multiply your sales and create more win-win successes by up-selling and cross selling.

24

CLOSING

❦

One salesman said to the other, *'I made some great presentations today.'*

The other replied, *'I didn't close any sales either.'* Are we in the presentation business? Or are we in the business to close a transaction with a positive outcome?

Some people feel that closing is where you have to put pressure on a person to buy. This really is not true. **A closing is a natural outcome of a good presentation.** In this, the salesperson has led the prospect towards the logic of a positive response to his request for an action or an order.

A good sales professional identifies a prospect's need and where it fits with his own product offering. He aims to satisfy that need with a product that provides the right solution. He proves that his solution does what he claims with concrete evidence. Then, he closes the transaction; ensures after-sales service; and walks away with a win-win situation.

When this is accomplished, the buyer has not only bought the product but has also bought into the seller of the product.

Just like beauty lies in the eyes of the beholder, the purchase price is determined by the perceived value to the buyer. In other words, a sales transaction can be defined as an exchange of perceived value/payment between the buyer and the seller.

Closing the Sale

Many people are afraid to close and they never ask for the order because they have a fear of being rejected. After making a good presentation, identifying the need and after providing the right solution, they hesitate to close. They say things like 'I will call you later,' or 'I will leave you with this information,' or 'Do you want to think about it?' or 'You can call me when you are comfortable.' This is self-destructive behavior.

All over the world, good organizations pay for results and not efforts. Of course, there cannot be any results without effort, but if the results are not in proportion to the effort, there is something wrong. We don't get paid for prospecting, building relationships and making presentations. We get paid to close the sale by securing or getting the agreement signed by the customer, getting the purchase order/application, along with a part of the payment. This means that qualitatively and quantitatively, there must be a benchmark for output.

At one time, sales people thought learning to close was the most important thing to learn in the selling process. Closing the sale is certainly very crucial because just making presentations and not closing would be self-defeating and a waste of time.

A good professional makes sure that every conversation, every gesture, every sentence gets you closer to the close. He sends positive verbal and non-verbal signals and observes the same signals from the customer. Fact-finding is a process of identifying a need to suggest the appropriate solution. This is done through a questioning technique. Good sales professionals, after asking a question, listen and look for clues to identify needs or compelling reasons to buy. These, in other words, are buying signals.

Many sales people don't make a good presentation and they use all kinds of manipulative tactics to close the sale and get an order.

My practice is to always summarize the benefits after the presentation, but before the close. Coming to a close without summarizing makes the presentation abrupt. It can destroy the chance of a close. One needs to be sensitive to the customer's feelings and then decide on the timing of the close. A summary should never exceed 3 benefits. Summarization should be as follows:

Mr Prospect, with your permission let me summarize our conversation with the major benefits: The way I see it, 3 major benefits flowing to your organization are – a . . . b . . . and . . . c . . .

Closing Skills or Techniques

There are many closing techniques. Eventually, each professional develops his own skills based on his level of comfort or discomfort. Some of the major closing techniques are as follows:

Trial Close

A trial close gives a person the choice between buying one product or another versus buying or not buying at all. A good professional, before closing, does the trial close. A trial close lets you feel or gives an indication as to how close you are to the actual close. It only asks for an opinion, not a decision. Trial closing is an effective way of getting feedback, whether the prospect likes the advantage offered by a product. It brings out objections, if any, into the open.

A trial close is testing the waters, while closing the sale is getting the commitment. Trial close is an opinion whereas a final close is a decision. Getting the commitment may not always end up in a signed document with a cheque, but it is as close to a commitment as you can get. A real commitment is only with a signed document and a cheque. Some examples of trial closes are:

- What do you think about this product?
- Assuming that it meets your need, when would you like it delivered?
- Which color do you prefer – blue or green?
- Would you like to have this delivered Saturday morning or Sunday evening?

Assumed Consent Close

Assumed consent close means that you ask questions and if the prospective customer goes along with you, answering all the questions, then you continue asking questions and say, 'Let's get the paperwork done. Do you mind if I ask you a few questions?' 9 times out of 10, if there is no resistance, you should go ahead. If you have made a good presentation, chances are good that you can go ahead.

During the days when I sold life insurance, I would have my applications on the table. You must have all applications/order forms on the table from the beginning of the presentation. At the time of the closing, never should you dig into the briefcase for applications/order forms as this creates suspicion. By having them on the table, you have done 2 things: (a) Psychologically, the prospect has gotten used to the paper sitting there, and (b) There is nothing new at the time of closing the sale that may make the client resist. Sample questions are:

- Do you use any middle initials?
- Do you want all correspondence at home or office?
- How would you like to make an investment, monthly or quarterly?
- How should we install the product?
- When will you be able to speak to your finance department about the investment plan?

If the prospect offers you no resistance whatsoever, then just complete the applications, swing it around and ask him to confirm the order.

Ben Franklin Close

This is very popular and is done by dividing a page into two columns. On one side is written the benefits of buying the product and on the other are the drawbacks of buying on the other (advantages and disadvantages). Here, you help the client list all the advantages, then ask him to write the disadvantages (all on his own). Now, count both sides and whichever is more, gets done. As a note of caution, one disadvantage may be heavier than twenty advantages.

The Silence Close

After you ask a closing question following a good presentation, you become silent but maintain eye contact without staring. Your silence is a big pressure on the client. Why does silence become a pressure on the prospect? Because now the ball is in his court and he has no choice but to make a decision. The decision being positive or negative would depend upon the quality of presentation and the little commitments that he has been giving along the way.

Sadly, the immature salesperson himself feels pressurized and nervous because of silence and he feels he must add on something. Not realizing that the moment he speaks up he has just destroyed his opportunity of closing a sale. He has just lifted the pressure from the prospect.

The Reverse Close

Here, the sales professional asks questions to eliminate the negatives and every negative eliminated brings us closer to a positive. Examples are:

* Is it my credibility that bothers you? Chances are the client says 'No'.
* Is it my company's credibility that bothers you? Again, he says 'No'.
* Is it the product that is not good? Here, we hope he says 'No'!

Every 'No' the client says, eliminates a negative and brings you closer to a positive close.

Pointed Close

Offering choices makes it easier for the buyer to take a decision. A good way of questioning is, 'Mr Prospect, if this takes care of your needs and falls within your budget, can we get the paperwork out of the way?' Just analyze this question. It establishes certain benchmarks very clearly:

* 'It takes care of your need' means we have a solution to the problem that is subject to your approval.
* 'If it falls into your budget.' Again, it means you have pre-empted the objection, 'I don't have the money,' or 'It's beyond my budget.'
* It is a very pointed question which needs a lot of confidence and a seasoned professional to ask.

Conditional Close

A conditional close is somewhat similar to a tentative close. It says, subject to my meeting these conditions you buy X, Y, or Z. 'If I could do . . . for you, would you like to get 5 dozen . . . for your company?

This is also for the undecided buyer who wants to buy but is hesitant to make a commitment. Here, a good salesperson would say, 'Tentatively, do we take it that you want the product to be delivered on the 28th of August?' The word 'tentatively' gives the customer comfort, because it gives him the feeling that everything is still subject to his final confirmation. A good professional may turn it around by saying, 'I take it as confirmed, unless it is cancelled.'

High Pressure Close

Many sales people are trained to put special emphasis and use high-pressure tactics to somehow get the client to sign the order and close the sale. This is unprofessional and manipulative. High pressure represents hard sell and pushy behavior. The objective here becomes get the order signed now without any concern for the customer or the company.

Hard-to-Get Close

Many clubs, to maintain exclusivity, limit the memberships to make it scarce and more desirable. For example, 'I realize you like this car much better but why don't you consider the one I showed you before. The monthly instalment on that one would be much lower and it seems more affordable.' Psychologically, many buyers would want to prove you wrong and make every effort to buy the higher priced one.

While selling life insurance, whenever someone gave me an objection like, '*I want to talk to my wife.*' I would say to him, '*Why would you want to push your wife to a corner? She might be embarrassed to say "yes", thinking it might sound greedy, and if she says "no", then would you not want to provide your family with the basics of food, clothing shelter, a good living and a proper education? You know, John, interestingly, I have heard some wives complaining about their husbands having too much life insurance. But have you ever heard a widow complain that her husband left her too much life insurance? Well, it really boils down to your decision, doesn't it? How would you like to make the investment, monthly or quarterly?'*

Don't Miss the Opportunity

The timing of a close is very important. When the customer asks, *'Does this come in red?'*, an untrained salesperson's answer is, *'Yes, it comes in red.'* If it does, he is likely to hear *'Oh, thanks for the information.'* The customer is gone and you have lost a selling opportunity. He may never come back. A good trained professional's response would be, *'Would you like to have it in red?'* If the customer says *'Yes,'* he has bought it because he has committed.

A good professional is constantly making and looking to receiving commitments or directing the conversation to get a commitment. Every small commitment eventually leads to the final commitment.

Why Close Now?

The client feels there is no urgency and he can do it later. Here, a professional, to motivate the undecided buyer, may offer an additional savings of say 5% or 10% if the client's cheque is received within a certain period. As a note of caution, don't use these things as gimmicks. If you do not stand by your words, you will lose credibility.

Turn a Setback into a Comeback

How to come back when you have lost the sale and the customer has said, 'No'?

This is what a good professional can say, 'Mr Prospect, as you know, my livelihood depends on my ability to sell. Obviously, your decision not to do business with us highlights my failing. I am answerable to my company and my manager. Could you help me by completing this form by writing 2 reasons for not doing business with us?'

Put the following form in front of him:

To the Manager
ABC Company

I have decided not to do business with your salesperson
because:
1.
2

Regards,
Mr XYZ

2 things can happen now. Either he could refuse to fill the form or he might just write 2 or 3 reasons. The moment he writes the reasons you can immediately say, 'Mr Prospect,

if we could resolve and address these 2 issues to your total satisfaction, then I imagine you would want to go ahead and own this product, wouldn't you?' If he says 'Yes', then you are back in business.

Reassure the Customer to Avoid Buyer's Remorse

What is buyer's remorse? Just the way a salesperson is under stress, so is the buyer because he does not want to make a wrong decision. After signing the application, he thinks a second time. Buyer's remorse comes from thinking: 'I hope I made the right decision.' A sale is not consolidated till the buyer has remorse. A good sales professional always reassures the client after the sale that the buyer has made the right decision. He reassures through a congratulation letter, reaffirming his/her company's commitment towards the customer.

In summary, once you've made a good presentation, focus on closing the sale. Consider the different ways of closing as you seek to draw the prospect naturally and positively towards making the commitment.

A good professional understands that selling is a process of mutual consent with a common destination. Hence, the closing becomes a question of when to buy, not whether to buy or not.

25

OBJECTION HANDLING

The buyer must feel comfortable that the purchase will benefit him and/or his organization. A buyer is always anxious to avoid a wrong or bad purchase which could end up in a loss of goodwill, time or money. This doubt or lack of confidence brings out objections.

Rarely can you find sales taking place without objections. In fact, objections help to close the sale because they point the salesperson in the direction that is most important to the buyer. Handling an objection is an integral part of the selling process. Objections are really the response to sales presentation. It shows us that the prospect has been touched emotionally. Objections are not rejections and should not be taken personally. Objections are only questions asking for more information. We need to understand the purpose of an objection and develop a system or process on how to respond or handle objections.

To a well-prepared professional, every objection is an opportunity to close. Here a good professional's persuasion skills come into play and the real selling starts when the prospect gives him an objection. Whenever a person gives an objection what he is really saying is, 'I am not satisfied . . . I am not convinced, try harder . . . give me more information, or a compelling reason to buy.' On hearing an objection, a good professional feels encouraged because this is his opportunity to convince and use his time-tested principles of selling.

Objections, by and large, fall into the following categories:

1. Unsure of the need – 'I am really not interested/I have no (perceived) need at all.'
2. Monetary terms – 'It's too expensive/The terms don't suit me.'
3. Lack of incentive to buy now – 'What's the rush or urgency?'
4. Happy with the existing position – 'I really don't need to change my suppliers/I don't have the time, send me some information.'
5. Lack of trust to buy from you/your company/your product.
6. 'I'll think it over/I want to think it over.'

Objections are typically generated through a lack of information being passed to the prospect, whether accidental or through complacence; through misunderstanding or through a lack of trust in the salesperson or the process.

Some objections are really reflex actions and stereotyped responses of buyers. Sometimes, potential customers do it on purpose, to test the competence and character of the salesperson. If it is handled properly people buy, and if not, then the prospect decides otherwise.

Many objections are the result of the way a salesperson conducts himself. His verbal and non-verbal language, his appearance, behavior, and mannerisms have an impact on either the generation or handling of an objection.

Some objections come from the prospect, while others are invitations to self-destruction from the salesperson himself. Prospects can sense all of the following about a salesperson:

- His belief in himself
- His products
- His company
- His attitude towards the prospect
- Whether he is commission-oriented or service-oriented

The purpose of handling objections is to reduce resistance and address concerns. There is a clear difference between objections, conditions and excuses. Sometimes, a resistance is spoken and voiced and sometimes it's not. The worst kind of objection one has is the one that is not brought out in the open, or hidden resistance – the one that actually prevents the buyer from taking action, but which is not verbalized. Some hidden objections may be:

- The prospect may not be the decision-maker, but he doesn't want to let the salesperson know.

- The prospect is somehow uncomfortable with the salesperson or vendor.
- The prospect doesn't really know what he wants to buy as yet.

The most important thing is to find out the real objection. Don't get distracted and sidetracked by petty issues or go off tangent. You may win the battle but lose the war. Whenever there is a hesitation from the prospect, it is very crucial to understand what is going through the mind of the prospect. One needs to probe further, tactfully. Some examples of probing questions are:

- What seems to be your concern?
- What causes your concern?
- Would you mind sharing your reservation?
- Why do you feel that way?

While handling objections, don't be defensive and start giving reasons why they should buy your product. We need to learn to handle one objection at a time. This puts the pressure back on the prospect.

Differentiate between an **objection** and a **condition**. When a buyer raises an objection he is really saying, 'I am not convinced yet. If I get convinced, probably I will buy it.' A condition is a circumstance that cannot be changed and prevents the buyer from making a purchase. No matter how good a salesperson I am, a condition cannot be changed and I cannot sell. If my seminar needs an investment of $3,000 and if the prospect's annual income is $6,000, no matter how good a selling job I do, he is unlikely to buy, unless his condition changes significantly.

A good professional should be prepared in advance to prevent objections. In the early days of selling life insurance, when I used to go out with my manager on a sales call, I would ask him what proposals I needed to carry with us. His answer used to be, 'Everything!' His reasoning was that when you are in front of a prospect and you uncover a need but are unable to propose a solution to the problem or end up giving an incomplete solution, what you have done is:

1. Prepared him, but left him unable to take a decision because of incomplete information.
2. Missed out on a closing opportunity.
3. By not being able to close right on the spot, you have left an opportunity for a competitor to come in and make a sale from your hot prospect!
4. Put a doubt in the mind of the client about your competence.

A good professional gets as much information as he can about the prospect in advance. He then goes prepared carrying with him proposals, applications, order forms, and referrals/testimonials. By proper planning and pre-empting, most objections can be prevented.

Pre-emption

Every time you make a presentation, there are one or two objections that keep coming again and again. So, instead of waiting for the prospect to raise these objections, a good sales professional pre-empts, brings them up in advance and converts them into benefit. For instance, if you know from experience that every sales call is getting you an objection on price, instead of waiting for the objection that your price is 3% higher, a good professional would say, 'Mr Prospect, our initial investment for the machine is 3% higher than most other brands, but your savings on running the equipment would be 10% annually, resulting in 50% saving within 5 years. Would you agree that 47% return on your initial investment of 3% differential would be a good return?'

Handling Objections

Steps to handle objections:

1. Confirm the objection
2. Isolate the objection
3. Empathize
4. Answer, respond or overcome the objection
5. Reconfirm the acceptance of your answer
6. Go for a trial close
7. Close

Clarify and confirm the objection

Clarify to make sure you understand and answer the real objection and not just the surface objections. Use phrases such as the following to get the clarity that you require:

- 'Just to clarify my thinking.'
- 'Let me make sure that I understand your concern.'
- 'Just to make sure that I can make the right recommendations, is this your concern . . .?'

After probing questions, one needs to listen very carefully. After that, reconfirm and clarify if you understood correctly. For example, the prospect says, '*It is too expensive.*' The salesperson replies, '*Could you elaborate a little bit please?*'

Isolate the Objection

Now, you want to find out if it is the real objection and if there is anything else that will prevent the prospect from placing an order. A sales professional would say:

- 'Just to clarify my thinking, it is the speed of the machine that concerns you, nothing else, am I right, sir?'
- 'If it wasn't for money or time, you would want to go along with this speed, is that right, sir?'
- If you answered the first one and you are ready to close, he will bring the second objection. In order to be able to close effectively you want to bring out all objections in the open. This way, you prevent any unpleasant surprises when the time comes to close.

Empathize

A degree of empathy with the prospect at this point can build a rapport and create a common feeling that diffuses the prospect's objection. Empathy helps you to put yourself in the other person's shoes. Empathy says 'I feel how you feel.' It propels you into action to relieve the other person of his pain. It helps you demonstrate the golden rule 'treat others the way you want to be treated.' Empathy decides the strength of the relationship.

Answer the objection

In my experience a very effective way to handle objections is to use the 'feel, felt and found' formula.

If the prospect says, 'I cannot afford it', evaluate if it is an objection or a condition.

The reply can be 'Mr Prospect, I can understand how you **feel** (shows empathy). Some other clients **felt** that way too (the potential client feels that he is not the only one) till they asked themselves the question – can they afford not to have it? They **found** that the increased productivity far outweighed the investment. Now, which one would you prefer, the red or blue.'

Reconfirm the Answer

Reconfirmation means that the objection has been answered completely to the prospect's satisfaction and he accepts it. This process is to ensure that the same objection does not erupt later at the time of closing.

- 'Does that answer your question?'
- 'Does that address your concern?'
- 'Does that make you feel comfortable?'
- 'Does that sound reasonable?'

Trial Close and Closing

Seize the moment now and go for the close. If you have answered the objections of the prospect satisfactorily, then this is the right time to close. Trial closes have been addressed in the previous chapters.

Handling Specific Objections

Why the urgency?

A potential buyer acts when he sees a gain from acting now versus a loss by delaying action. When you understand that the prospect wants your product, but hesitates to make the purchase now, the salesperson can say:

+ 'Mr Prospect, if we receive the investment 10 days prior to the dispatch of the equipment, you have an additional saving of 10%.'
+ 'Mr Prospect, if you place your order now, we will offer you complimentary service for 6 months.'

Caution: Keep in mind that you should tell the truth and stick to a policy of ethical behavior. The objective is not to manipulate and only focus on getting the sale landed, but to make the prospect act now. If you use it as a gimmick, you will still end up losing credibility.

The 'Yes . . . but' Technique

I have seen many sales trainers teaching the 'yes . . . but' approach to objection handling. This is not one I recommend. What does this approach mean? Here, the salesperson says:

+ 'I agree with you, but . . .'

The question is, did I really agree? The moment I said 'but' the agreement is conditional or erased. This approach sounds manipulative. If there is an agreement in place, then why is the 'but' required?

How can we replace this approach? Replace the 'but' with 'and' or 'in addition to that.' For example:

* 'I agree with you and could you please . . .'
* 'I agree with you and in addition to that could you please . . .'

Monetary Objections

If the prospect replies, '*It is too expensive . . .*', a good professional would ask, '*Things are relative. It is too expensive as compared to what?*' He could further add:

* 'Low price sounds nice momentarily, but to deal with poor quality day-after-day becomes problematic. Mr Prospect, I am sure, you are aware of the difference between price and cost. Most of our clients find that the cost of breakdown, headaches and frustration are not worth the saving of a few dollars.'
* Always try to give three reasons. Psychologically, odd numbers work better than even numbers. I cannot explain why, but they do! Less than three may be too little to convince and more than three is over-doing it.
* 'Even though our investment seems somewhat higher, I am sure you would like to know the three major reasons why people prefer to do business with us.'
* 'Mr Prospect, as you know I have a choice to sell any product, including my competitor's with the lower price. I am sure you would like to know why I feel comfortable in selling this product.'

* 'Mr Prospect, do you mind if I ask whether your company takes pride in being the cheapest in the market or in giving the best value for money?' or 'We are like you – we take pride in giving value; which one would you prefer, red or blue?'

When a person says the price is too high, he might be saying many things:

* 'I do not have the money' or his perceived value is too low,
* 'I am not getting my money's worth,' or
* He might be saying it is too high compared with the competitor's price.

Unless we clarify which one it is out of the three, we will not be able to answer objections correctly. The money objection can be handled in several ways. For example, the salesperson can ask, 'How high is the difference between us and the competitors?'

Suppose the client says, '10% or a $100 on a total purchase of $1,000.'

This can be answered by saying 'Sir, how long do you plan to keep this equipment?'

He answers, '6 years.'

Now, 6 years translates close to $18 a year, which means $1.50 a month, further into 35 cents a week, that is, less than 5 cents a day. Now, a professional will ask the potential client, 'Sir, is your peace of mind because of our reliable service not worth 5 cents a day? Which one would you prefer, red or green?'

The monetary difference is insignificant and ridiculous, but psychologically, gaining peace of mind is very significant. I repeat the old saying – **I would rather explain my higher price once than apologize for poor quality forever.**

As another example, if the prospect says, 'I am going to buy something cheaper,' the suggested response is 'Mr Prospect, I understand how you feel. Have you ever bought something just because it was cheaper and later wished that you had made a decision to own something of better quality?'

'I had a bad experience with your company.'

The client's objection is 'I had a bad experience in the past.' Now this can mean anything – either he had a bad experience with the product, company or with someone in the organization. We need to find out what exactly is the problem.

A professional will approach by saying, 'First of all, I apologize for the inconvenience that you had to face. Do you mind sharing it with me, so that I can rectify the problem and ensure that it doesn't happen again?' Now, it is the salesperson's responsibility to find out if it is a legitimate complaint, if yes, then it should be addressed and removed permanently.

There is another way of handling this kind of objection and that is after apologizing and acknowledging, the salesperson could ask the customer, 'Has any customer of your company ever put forward a complaint like this?' What do you think

> **I would rather explain my higher price once than apologize for poor quality forever.**

the answer would be? Chances are that it has probably happened in every organization. Now, whatever answer the prospect gives, just say, 'That is exactly how we plan to handle this.'

Another approach, 'Mr Prospect, first of all, I apologize for the inconvenience. I am sure you would agree with me that we all have at, some time or the other, eaten something which made us sick. Of course we haven't stopped eating after that. I assure you that this problem will not happen again and that you will be totally satisfied with our services.'

Another way of answering is, 'Mr Prospect, please accept my apologies. With your due permission, I will ensure that things are set right and to your total satisfaction.' It is very important to ensure that the apology is not only lip service but must be sincere. If there is a genuine concern, it must be addressed too.

When the prospect's objection is that he feels there is a lack of credibility in the supplier, we need to convince the prospect that the people and the organization that he is dealing with today are totally customer-focused.

To prove the authenticity and establish credibility, the salesperson can do the following:

- Show testimonial letters
- Use centers of influence
- Give factual data such as how long you have been in the business, market share, volumes and number/percentage of repeat buyers.

'I like the other product better.'

'I understand how you **feel**. Some other people **felt** the same too, till they **found** that . . . and that our service gave them peace of mind. How many would you like to own, 3 or 4?'

'I want it, I need it, but I am not totally comfortable.'

A professional would ask, 'Mr Prospect, what could I do to make you feel comfortable? I will be more than happy to do it, so please tell me.'

'I want to think it over'/The Indecisive Buyer

An indecisive buyer is one who hesitates in making a decision. The easiest escape for this kind of customer is to say, 'I want to think it over.' Why does a person say this? There are three reasons:

1. He doesn't have the courage to say no to you.
2. This is a polite way of getting rid of you without really refusing to buy.
3. A person genuinely needs help to make up his mind.

So whenever a person says, *'I want to think it over . . .'*, most sales people are unable to handle this objection because there is nothing concrete to respond to. A good professional knows how to handle the situation. Here is how he would handle it.

He would say, *'Obviously you don't want to make a mistake, that is why you want to think it over, isn't it?'*

The prospect says, *'That is true.'* The client also feels that you are empathizing with him.

A good professional knows how to come back by asking the second question, *'Which part is it that you want to think over?'*

1. 'Is it my credibility?'   The prospect says 'No'
2. 'Is it my company's?'   He says 'No'
   credibility
3. 'Is it my product?'   He again says 'No'
4. 'Is it the investment?'   He says 'No'

Every time he says 'no' it means he does not have any problem with that issue. However, if the prospect says, *'I have a problem with the price. It is too much,'* then a good professional will isolate the problem.

He would ask, *'Sir, if it was not for the money you would go ahead, wouldn't you?'*

The prospect says, *'Of course.'*

The moment you identify the hidden objection which is 'money,' you can now handle it in many ways, for example, by giving choices for instalment plans.

* 'If an instalment could be worked out, what kind of monthly budget would you be comfortable with?'

One can always handle a specific objection rather than an abstract or unknown objection. Other ways of responding to this kind of objection are (feel, felt, found formula) as follows:

'I understand how you feel. Mr Prospect, there are some things in life that no matter how many times we think, we always get the same answer. For example, if your car's color is red, no matter how many times you are asked, it is still the same. Similarly, someone asks you your date of birth, no matter how many times you think, you are always going to come up with the same answer.'

'Mr Prospect, I read once that there are only three kinds of people in the world:

     i.   Those who make things happen.
    ii.   Those who watch things happen.
   iii.   Those who wonder what happened.

I am sure you fall under the first category, those who make things happen. Which one would you prefer, red or blue?'

Some sales professionals pull out a $100 bill from their pocket and say 'Mr Prospect, do you have a $100 bill in your pocket? Could I please see it? Every day that you delay the decision, it costs you $100. I am sure none of us wants to pull out $100 from our pocket and waste it.'

'Mr Prospect, whenever we want to think it over, we are really wondering:

+ Do I need it?
+ Can I afford it?

And you have answered both these questions comfortably. How many would you like to have, 3 or 4?'

'Mr Prospect, many products are similar and do the same things. The real difference is the people's commitment and integrity behind the product. All I can say is I am not here just to get your business but to earn it by providing quality service. Which would you prefer, red or blue?

Mr Prospect, I understand how you feel. Some other people felt that way too, till they found that for 5 cents a day differential, they would prefer to have peace of mind. How many would you like to have – 3 or 4?

The Brother-in-law Objection

Suppose the prospect gives you an objection that his brother-in-law is in the business and he cannot buy from you. Now the question comes – if the brother-in-law is in the same business, does he have an advantage over you? The answer is yes, of course. But the big question is how long or how much of an advantage does he have? Only once!

Now evaluate this scenario: Suppose the prospect buys from his brother-in-law (he is in the same business as the sales professional is). Now if the brother-in-law does not send the client the right product or does not provide good quality service or reliability and dependability after the sale, the client starts losing money or feels it is hurting his goodwill. Would the client continue to do business with his brother-in-law? The answer is no. After the first sale is made, and if the brother-in-law messes up, it becomes a level playing field. The advantage is over. The rules of the game are very clear, either perform or get out.

What if the brother-in-law is providing quality product and great service? In that case, a person can always ask a buyer, 'All far-sighted business people keep a stand-by arrangement. Let me be your stand-by arrangement for whatever reason. If something goes wrong at some point of time, at least I will be there to help you meet your commitment. And I'm sure, as a far-sighted business person, you would like to have that, wouldn't you?' Which far-sighted person would say 'No' to that?

Turning a Negative into a Positive

How can you change or reverse an objection in your favor? I recall from my insurance days, when someone gave the objection that *'My cousin takes care of it'*, my answer used to be *'I understand how you feel. Some other people also felt that way till they found that . . . Mr Prospect, insurance and financial matters are of a very personal nature and sometimes people are reluctant to share personal information with close relatives. Could we meet next Monday morning or would Tuesday evening be better?'*

Keep in mind that the best salesperson in the world cannot sell 100%. Hence, our objective is to get our batting average up.

'I'm satisfied with my current supplier.'

The key thing here is to make sure that you get a small order and that you start building a relationship with the client. You never know what might be happening inside the existing supply arrangement. People may feel satisfied, but they may also be missing some of the qualities of your product without even knowing it. This objection can be handled in a couple of different ways.

The first is to empathize with the client on how he feels and how his loyalty is to be appreciated. However, add, 'We find most visionary businesses, as a good business practice, always keep a stand-by, reliable source of supply. Why don't you place a trial order/small order with us? Try us out so that we can become your standby source.'

The second way of handling is to ask, 'How do you rate your current supplier on a scale of 1 to 10?' If he says anything less than 10, right away you can say, 'Sir, what is it that needs to be done to make your supplier get the rating of 10?' That will give you a clue to come back and make a sale.

'You are located too far away/it is inconvenient to buy from you.'

Almost 90% of the solutions lie in properly identifying the problems. Ask, 'Mr Prospect, do I understand that your concern is that the time taken for us to provide you the service is too much?' If he says 'Yes', you have just converted distance to time taken. Further, ask your client what in his opinion is a good response time. If he says 2 or 3 hours, just say, 'Well, if we can respond within that time-frame, then we can proceed further, can't we?'

A good professional does not just stop at the point of having answered questions. His stopping point always would be asking for the order. In the above example, he could ask by saying 'Mr Prospect, your real concern or question is how much response time would it take in case of a problem, not the distance of our office, am I right?' If he says 'Yes', then a good professional would ask, rather than answering at this point 'What would be an acceptable response time to you?' Suppose, he says 3 hours or 1 day, then an effective response would be 'If we meet your criteria of response time, then how many PCs would you to like to have, 3 or 4?' or 'How would you like to make your investment – monthly or annual?'

As a note of caution – you must meet the criteria or his requirement. A good professional would not lie or not meet his commitment.

Is it a Real Objection?

After satisfying the objections, clarify and confirm that the objection, is in fact, answered to the client's satisfaction by saying, 'Does this satisfy your concern?' or, 'Does this answer your question?' Remember that some people raise objections only to start an argument and nothing else. They may not be genuine buyers. Not having a valid objection may work to your advantage if you just bypass it. However, if it is a valid objection, the customer will bring it up and then you can answer it in the manner explained above. Never lie. If you don't have an answer, just say, 'I am sorry I don't have the answer. I will come back to you', and ask for time. Then you must revert in that specific time, otherwise you will lose credibility. Don't ever get into an argument. Don't feel frustrated or annoyed. Don't get defensive or offensive. Never raise your voice.

Address objections when you find a hidden concern

Objection raised	Concern/doubt	Solution/ Reassurance
Cost too much or price too high.	Unsure of value or is it really worth the price?	Need value confirmation
What's the urgency or why now?	Why should I decide now?	Show him the loss in waiting or a benefit by acting now
I am happy with my present supplier.	Why should I change?	Give him the benefit of changing or adding a second source.
Bad experience with your company.	He is afraid of loss.	Show proof that you have improved.
I will talk to my advisor.	He may not be the decision-maker, or looking to justify his decision.	Give reassurance or demonstrate risk reduction.
I want to think it over.	Afraid of making wrong decision.	Give reassurance.

Accept that objections are inbuilt and you know that they are going to come up in every situation, no matter what.

Competent professionals are skillful enough to turn an objection into an opportunity to close. They turn setbacks into comebacks. Remember, wise people build homes with stones that are thrown at them.

Remember, wise people build homes with stones that are thrown at them.

26

NEGOTIATION OR HAGGLING

❧

Generally, all buyers try to get the best value for money. Hence, they start by attempting to negotiate. There is a difference between negotiation and haggling: negotiation is trying to arrive at a win-win situation which comes down to finding a place where both parties believe that they are getting value for money, whereas haggling ends up being perceived by both parties, as a losing proposition. It results in discontentment and sour relationships. For all future dealings both parties remain permanently on guard.

For example, in a car sale/purchase, the sticker price is the starting point for both parties. The buyer asks, *'What better can you do?'* and the seller says, *'That is the best I can do.'* They are both testing each other and now the process starts about who is going to melt first. The buyer starts by either reducing the price or asking for accessories and the seller wants to hold on, but gives in a little. The buyer haggles and gets some more. The seller haggles and gives in a little more and eventually they strike a bargain somewhere. After they have signed the contract and the car is delivered, the buyer feels he could have gotten a better bargain and the seller feels he gave away too much. Both parties end up dissatisfied.

Once in Nigeria, I was doing a program for Lufthansa, which happens to be one of my clients. While I was there, I went to a flea market with my host to purchase some local handicrafts. He told me that once I liked something I should tell him in his ear, without pointing at the product. This way the vendor wouldn't know that I liked it and he could bargain on the price. The conversation went as follows:

Friend:	*Look, we are serious about buying this product, what is your price?*
Vendor:	*$100.*
Friend:	*That is your price. Give me a better price.* (No counter offer was made.)
Vendor:	*$95.*
Friend	*Give me an even better price.*
Vendor:	*$90.*
Friend:	*No. Give me your best price.*
Vendor:	*$85.*
Friend:	*This is too much. I am serious about buying. Give me your best price.*
Vendor:	*$80.*
Friend:	*Give me your last price.*
Vendor:	*$80. I cannot come down any more.*

At this point we started to walk away but the vendor called us back.

Vendor:	*Come back. I'll give it to you for $75.*
Friend:	*Give me your last price.*
Vendor:	*I've already given you my last price. It is $75.*
Friend:	*That was your last price. Now give me your last, last price,*

(No counter offer was made up to this point,)

| Vendor: | *Okay. Last and final price – $65.* |

(Before making any counter offer, he has already brought him down 35%.)

Friend:	(Pulls out money.) *Look, I am a serious buyer. If you are really serious, give me your last and final price.*
Vendor:	*$63.*
Friend:	*That is too much.* (Every time he asked him to lower his price, without making any counter offer.) *I will give you my last price – $30.* (He hands him $30.)
Vendor:	*Oh, what are you saying? You have just insulted me. Here is your money. It is too low and I can't sell it for that.*

At this point, we started to walk away again. He called us back. The haggling went on, the vendor asking for $63, coming down to $45. He offered him $35 and finally the deal was closed at $37.

When we left, we were all dissatisfied. We felt we could have got it for less and the vendor felt he sold it for too little.

This is called haggling and peddling. This is not negotiation and selling. The seller knows that haggling is a way of life and the buyer knows that if he doesn't haggle, he will be cheated. Both look to outsmart each other. If your way of doing business is the same as in the example above, you will keep looking for the next victim and never build a good business.

A good negotiation has some very clear ground rules. It starts with:

1. Mutual respect
2. No interruptions
3. Handling one issue at a time
4. Coming to agreements on minor matters quickly
5. Starting to build on your points of agreement
6. Separate negotiable and non-negotiable items
7. Priorities

Some Tips on Negotiating

- Observe the verbal and non-verbal language of the other party. Your own verbal and non-verbal signals should reflect a positive attitude.
- Don't argue. Avoid rude and loud behavior.
- Be assertive not aggressive. Assertiveness means firmness with politeness while aggressiveness is firmness without politeness.
- Use hard arguments with soft words, not soft arguments and hard words.

- Maintain eye contact without staring. Eye contact shows confidence and trust whereas staring shows that you're daring and challenging.
- Stay focussed on the topic, don't go off-track. Keep asking questions to uncover the real concern without being interrogative.
- Don't blame anyone because that makes the environment tense immediately.
- Avoid sarcasm.
- Accept responsibility.
- A good negotiation does not reveal your weakness.

For example, if you have to meet a quota by the end of the month, don't show your desperation or you might lose. During negotiation, don't make emotional decisions that you may have a problem carrying out later.

A good sales professional realizes that his ability to persuade the other person to his way of thinking, logically and emotionally, should be used without offending. Someone once said, 'He tells you go to hell and you look forward to it.'

27

GOAL SETTING

Set Goals

Top sales professionals in the world are ones who set targets, remain focussed and are driven by goals. They are result-oriented, not just activity-oriented. They realize that while there are no results without activity, all activities do not give results. Hence, they choose their activities very carefully, based on priorities and make sure they get the result.

Goals are important because they give a sense of direction. How can you reach a destination that you have not defined? There is a lot of wisdom in these three words – **destination, determines direction.** Studies show that less than 3% people have written goals, 97 % people don't. Talent will get you to your destination, provided you know where it is.

'Great minds have purposes, others have wishes.'

– Washington Irving

If goals are so important, why don't most people set goals?

A major reason is the lack of clarity on definition of a goal. Most people confuse dreams with goals. They have dreams and they think they have goals. Goals are dreams with a deadline, a clear direction and a plan of action.

Dreams and wishes are nothing more than desires. Desires are weak. Dreams become goals only when they are supported by:

**Direction   Dedication   Determination
Discipline   Deadlines**

There are many reasons why people don't set goals:

1. A pessimistic attitude – Looking for the pitfalls rather than the possibilities.
2. Fear of failure – Thinking 'what if I don't make it?' Subconsciously, people feel that if they don't set goals they can't fail. Many a time, fear of failure is a much bigger deterrent in life than failure itself.

Most people confuse dreams with goals. They have dreams and they think they have goals. Goals are dreams with a deadline, a clear direction and a plan of action.

---

3. Fear of success – Low self-image or fear of having to live up to their success causes some people to fear success. Let me explain what it means. Many people sabotage their own success. Have you noticed there are some people in this world who's life script is such that the moment they are about to achieve their goal or the goal is within grasp, something goes wrong at the last minute every time. Logically and externally they aspire to win but somewhere inside, their self-limiting belief prevents them from achieving their goal. Invariably, their belief comes true.

   In one sentence, losers are afraid of winning whereas winners are not afraid of losing.

4. A lack of ambition – A result of our value system and lack of desire to live a fulfilled life. Our limited thinking prevents us from progress. To illustrate, let me give you an example. There was a fisherman who, every time he caught a big fish, would throw it back into the river, keeping only the smaller ones. A man watching this unusual behavior asked the fisherman why he was doing this. The fisherman replied, 'Because I have a small frying pan.' Most people never make it in life because they are carrying a small frying pan. That is limited thinking.

5. A fear of rejection – Worrying that, 'If I don't make it, what will the others say?' Our low self-esteem makes us believe

> **Losers are afraid of winning whereas winners are not afraid of losing.**

that other people's opinions are more important than ours. This shows lack of confidence not arrogance.

6. Procrastination – 'Someday, I will set my goals.' These tie in with a lack of ambition. People confuse complacence with contentment. Contentment is good, complacence is not.

7. Low self-esteem – A person is not internally driven and has no inspiration.

8. Ignorance of importance of goals – nobody taught them and they never learnt the importance of goal-setting.

9. A lack of knowledge about goal-setting – People don't know the mechanics of setting goals. They need a step-by-step guide so that they can follow a system.

It is not wishing alone, but passion that turns dreams into reality. Goal-setting is a series of steps. The components of goal-setting are similar to that of a plane ticket. When you buy a plane ticket, what does it say? It gives time, date, class of travel, the departure and destination cities, price, etc.

A good sales professional is focussed and goal-oriented. He has time-bound targets. Goals can be:

Short-term – up to 1 year
Medium-term – up to 3 years
Long-term – up to 5 years

Long-term goals can also go beyond 5 years, but generally if they are beyond 5 years, we consider them a purpose of life. What is purpose? A lifetime goal is called a purpose. A purpose is important because without it, you are likely to develop tunnel vision, where you are obsessed only with achieving your immediate goals. Our short, mid- and long-term goals must lead us to our purpose. This is called alignment. All our goals must be divided into **needs and wants**. Needs are stronger than wants. For example, I need a car but I want a Mercedes. The need is for a car but the desire is to own a Mercedes.

Most people are vague about what are their major objectives in life. They think that 'I want to be successful, happy and make a good living' are objectives. These are all wants and none of them are clear goals. Goals must be SMART:

S   Specific
M   Measurable
A   Achievable
R   Realistic
T   Time Bound

'I want to lose weight.' Is this statement a goal? The answer is it is only a wish, not a goal. Why? This is because it is neither specific nor measurable nor time-bound. However, if I said 'I want to lose 10 pounds by XYZ date or in 45 days,' that is a specific, time-bound and a measurable goal. Is the statement, 'I want to lose 10 pounds in 1 day,' a goal? The answer is no, because this goal is both unrealistic and not achievable. Between realistic and achievable, there is a little overlapping. If a goal is within reach, does it motivate us? The answer is no, it doesn't. If it is within our grasp and easy to reach, it gives us no sense of achievement/accomplishment even if we achieve it. Therefore, goals must be **stretch** goals. They must be slightly out of reach but not out of sight.

Goals out-of-reach are motivating, goals out-of-sight are de-motivating.

'Life is hard by the yard, but by the inch, it's a cinch.'
— *Gean Gordon*

Larger goals are more easily achieved if they are broken into small ones. How do you achieve yearly goals? The same way you eat an elephant! The answer is: one bite at a time!

Mechanics to achieve your goals:

Divide your yearly goal into the smallest common denominator.

1. Semi-annual	2. Quarterly	3. Monthly
4. Weekly	5. Daily	6. Hourly

Write down your goals and read them daily. Pen down your yearly and hourly goals on a sheet of paper in your office just to make sure you keep meeting your hourly goals. If you meet your hourly goals, you will automatically meet your weekly, monthly and yearly goals, but if you are behind on your hourly goal, it disturbs the timing of other goals as well. People who say, 'I did not do it today but will make up for it tomorrow' cannot and will not do it because their commitment is missing. Time is a perishable commodity. Ask a hotelier if they have not sold a room for one night. Can the other 364 nights cover the loss for that one night? No. It is gone forever.

An ancient Indian sage was teaching his disciples the art of archery. He put a wooden bird as the target and asked his disciples

> **Goals out-of-reach are motivating, goals out-of-sight are de-motivating.**

to aim at the eye of the bird. At first, the disciple was asked to describe what he saw. He said, *'I see the trees, the branches, the leaves, the sky, the bird and its eye.'*

The sage asked this disciple to wait. Then, he asked the second disciple the same question and he replied, *'I only see the eye of the bird.'*

The sage said, *'Very good. Now shoot.'* The arrow was bang on target.

The moral is, unless we focus, we cannot achieve our goal. It is hard to streamline our thoughts and concentrate, but it is a skill that can be learnt.

A good sales professional will set his target very clearly. For example, if a person needs to make a $1,000 a week and his average commission is $350, that means he needs to make 3 sales a week. In order to make 3 sales a week, he has to make 10 sales presentations face-to-face. In order to make 10 presentations, he is required to make 15 appointments a week. This is because he leaves room for cancellations in case of contingencies or unforeseen reasons. In order to have 15 appointments, he needs to speak to 50 decision-makers a week. In order to speak to 50 decision-makers a week, he needs to make 150 calls a week.

A good sales professional is aware of his closing ratios and activity level. There are no shortcuts. In order to double up his sales or income from $1,000 to $2,000 a week, he can do only 3 things:

1. Double up his activity making 30 appointments and keeping 20, closing 6 sales with each sale giving him $350.

2. Keep the same number of appointments (10), but double up the size of his commission to $700.
3. Improve his closing ratio, from 3 out of 10 to 6 out of 10.

The first option may not help because even if he can increase the number of appointments from 10 to 12 or 15, it has its limitations, because eventually there are only so many hours per day and you cannot stretch time beyond 24 hours. You can only see so many people and no more. The best way would be:

* To optimize the number of appointments.
* Multiply the volume to double, triple or more per sale.
* To improve the closing ratio.

All three combined, along with time optimization would be the recipe to success. The ideal scenario would be to have 20 presentations a week with a 60% closing ratio or (twelve sales) with double the value ($700 per sale) resulting in $8,400 commission per week.

The above awareness will help and enhance output and make a person set appropriate goals. Without this knowledge, one could be working hard yet not be successful. If that is the case, then you need to re-evaluate your activity and competence levels.

Activity is not the same as accomplishment

'Do not confuse motion and progress. A rocking horse keeps moving but does not make any progress.'

– Alfred A. Montapert

The action plan should clarify what to do, when to do, who will do it, and by when. A good professional always identifies and breaks down his activity into results. For example, how many phone calls do you need to make to get an appointment, how many appointments to a sale, how many sales (closing ratios) leading to referrals and new contacts.

Increase your income by 52% each year

Does it sound impossible that you could increase your income by 52% every year?

Did you ever realize that it is a lot easier to change 1% in a 100 different areas than to change 100% in any one area? That means, if we just make 1% overall improvement per week in our behavior activity and productivity, our annual growth would be 52% a year (figuratively speaking).

Don't start calculating these percentages. They will never add up. Catch the spirit! Remember, there are some people who keep dissecting the roots while others eat the fruits! Just imagine what this can amount to compounding every year in 5 years.

All you have to do is make a 1% overall improvement per week. How can you achieve this improvement annually?

- Read your goals twice a day.
- Plan your day 1 week in advance.
- Read 30 minutes every day before going to bed.

> **Remember, there are some people who keep dissecting the roots while others eat the fruits!**

- Listen to a motivational audio CD while driving.
- Evaluate each sales call immediately by asking 2 questions:
  - What are the things that I should have done and I didn't?
  - What are the things that I did do but should not have done?
- Make every person feel important about themselves.

'The men who try to do something and fail are infinitely better than those who try to do nothing and succeed.'

– Lloyd Jones

A good sales professional is focussed, yet he is not blind to what is going on around him. Big dreams act like magnets, attracting you closer to your destination. It takes the same effort and time to sell a small-ticket item that it takes to sell a big-ticket item. The only difference is a few zeros at the end. A person who is serious about achieving his goal always has a time-bound action plan broken down into small segments.

Think big, dream big, sell big.

28

MANAGING TIME

Parkinson's Law – Work expands to fill the time available for its completion.

To the sales professional, his stock in trade is his time. He does not waste his time in dilly-dallying, gossiping, chit-chatting or drinking endless cups of tea or coffee. A good sales professional prioritizes his work and ensures that his time is spent on important matters and with important people.

Time management is only a name given to life management

It may be the best time or the worst for anything but this is the only time we have. A good professional values his time and puts a price tag on himself. He doesn't sit at the reception for 2 hours, waiting for the prospect to see him. Within a matter of 10 to 15 minutes, he walks up to the secretary and says, 'It seems Mr X is busy at this time, I have another appointment to go to. Let us set up another time that will be mutually more convenient.' The key word here is 'mutually' because you respect your own and the other person's time.

Time is a perishable commodity, yet very few people value it as a precious resource. You use it or lose it. A commission salesperson gets compensated for results not reasons. You get paid for accomplishments not activities. **Productivity depends on the effective use of time.**

People, who waste valuable minutes, eventually lose hours and days not realizing the loss till it is too late. Each one of us gets a daily deposit of 1,440 minutes, every 24 hours. It's up to us to use it, lose it or abuse it. Unlike a bank account, you cannot carry forward a time balance in your life.

> **You get paid for accomplishments not activities.**

If sales people do not have their appointments fixed in advance then they wake up unemployed every day. And sadly, many do. A selling schedule must be planned in advance. Many sales people waste time deciding who to call next. Some sales people are excellent professionals with great sales ability but are unable to organize their time. Does a person need a doctorate to understand that **losing precious time is really a crime against oneself?**

Utilizing time properly is a matter of two things – **prioritizing and self-discipline.**

> **Unlike a bank account, you cannot carry forward a time balance in your life.**

When I was in the insurance business, I remember Thursday evening used to be my advance planning time for the week ahead. I would spend a few hours making phone calls to set all my appointments. When I started, my average was that I made about 150 calls to speak to 50 decision-makers to set up appointments with them. 100 calls would be those which nobody answered or where the person I was looking for was not there. Out of the 50 people I spoke to, I would end up making 15 appointments to meet face-to-face. Even though, practically, it was possible to keep only 12 appointments, I would still make 15 because invariably, 10-15% appointments get cancelled for some reason or the other. People who are serious in meeting their goals always keep a cushion for the unforeseen, which means they see the unforeseen in advance. Result-oriented people plan for the unplanned.

The unprofessional and disorganized show gross disrespect for their own and other people's time.

Respect Time

A good professional understands that like an arrow shot, spoken words and time lost never come back. Hence, time loss is life loss. Life management is nothing more than managing priorities in life. When someone calls me for dinner, sometimes I tell them that I am already committed and so will be unable to come. In unsaid words, I am really saying that my other engagements are more important. We need to make choices, the higher priority takes precedence. This is not pompous

> **Result-oriented people plan for the unplanned.**

behavior, but we need to know when to say 'yes', and when to say 'no'.

Some suggestions for effective utilization of time

1. Make every effort to qualify your prospect.
2. Divide your prospects into three categories: hot leads, lukewarm and cold leads – Go after the hot leads first, then the lukewarm and then the cold. This sets priorities.

   Don't waste too much time on the one off 'pie in the sky' big sale. I remember while selling insurance, if there was a big sale in the pipeline, my manager always cautioned me that a big sale should always be treated as a bonus. If the big sale happens, it is a lottery. If it doesn't, do not lose your bread and butter for an imaginary feast. What I mean is that many a time, people keep looking for the big sale to become millionaires overnight. What they don't realize is that it may not happen at all. Good professionals continue consistently on their growth path. The key word is consistency to avoid both feast and famine.
3. Don't allow unscheduled visitors to drop in – These are people who don't do their own job and like to waste other people's time. If you ask them what brings them to you they will say, 'I just dropped in to say hello and have a cup of tea with you.' They will waste an hour and they think they sat for only 5 minutes with you. Is that what we are getting paid for? In a situation like this, they are not at fault; in fact, they come in only if you allow them. It only shows that you lack commitment yourself.

4. Don't make unnecessary friendly calls and waste other people's time as well as yours – If you have time in your schedule between meetings, think about how you can efficiently meet new prospects and do some fact-finding.

5. Through your actions, always let your customer know you respect their time – Always confirm your appointments in advance. This does not mean that the person is egoistic or snobbish, just that you have shown the courtesy due to a client.

6. Have a good night's sleep – A well-rested body and mind function energetically the next day. It will help you increase productivity and will give your prospects a better vibe.

7. Keep yourself physically fit.

8. Paperwork and follow-up are two things that sales people find difficult to handle. However, without a logical follow-up system, there is no way we can stay in the profession successfully. The following filing system worked well for me – create 31 files dated 1 to 31 and when follow-up is required, put it on the appropriate file. Then, every day, you will automatically know who has to be followed up on that day. When follow-up is required after talking to a potential client or after sending a proposal, if it is not done the sale is lost and all that time wasted. If they are followed up too late or after too long, the client might have forgotten. This would put the salesperson out of business. Relying on memory alone is a recipe for disaster. Hence, it is crucial to develop your own external memory jogger system that would ensure a timely follow-up. The key word here is external. Whether it is a dairy, planner or a prioritized carry forward to-do list or a color-coded

chart, or whatever you are comfortable with, it must be a fool-proof system in writing.

9. Utilizing unproductive time – convert waiting time from wasted time to productive time. Examples of waiting time are:

   i. At the client or doctor's office, clinic or home
   ii. Driving time or travel time

Good professionals utilize this time in listening to motivational messages or reading a book that would enhance their knowledge. I used to rehearse my presentation while driving. If you drive a few hours a day and listen to a motivational CD, you could probably end up with a qualification equivalent to a college or university graduate.

A good business operation certainly needs to consider the relationship of time, revenue and profitability. This is where the 80:20 rules come into play. One needs to identify the accounts with the most potential and apportion time, based on return on an investment, to be able to generate profit.

A good sales professional should ensure that he optimizes selling time rather than getting into time-consuming administrative functions. Probably, most sales people, especially managers, interface 20% of their time with their customers and spend 80% available time on administrative functions or possibly correcting their own and others' mistakes. If we want to be more effective, we need to live by the following two principles:

1. **Do the right thing first time, every time.**

2. **Invest 80% of your time on revenue generation.**

If you waste time, time will waste you.

If you observe the way people walk, you can notice that different people walk differently. Some walk briskly and others drag their feet. The person walking briskly knows exactly where he is going and by when he has to reach there. The person who is dragging his feet is going nowhere. One makes things happen and the other is waiting for the things to happen. One is living and the other is marking time.

Your Time/Life Control Sheet

Maintain a time log for the next 7 days to identify your current usage and wastage of time. Do it in the slot of 30 minutes as follows:

Name: Date:

Time	Activity	Comments: Satisfied/ dissatisfied with usage of time	Reason for satisfaction/ dissatisfaction	Commitment for better usage of time
8.00–8.30				
8.30–9.00				
9.00–9.30				

Evaluate the above to identify the 5 productive things you want to do more of and 5 unproductive things that you want to avoid.

If you waste time, time will waste you.

An organized schedule has a pay-off. An unorganized schedule you have to pay for. Effective time management is a commitment that needs self-discipline. Planning daily activities shows professionalism and gives a competitive advantage to those who do it.

People who are goal-oriented have a competitive advantage over others. If you are a long-term player and want to succeed as a professional, then being fully committed to setting and achieving your goals and measuring your progress on a daily basis is the recipe for success. The key words are 'measuring your progress on a daily basis.' Because nothing magical is going to happen at the last moment unless consistent effort has gone in advance.

We all have waiting time in life – winners wait for their destination and losers wait for their destiny.

Nothing magical is going to happen at the last moment unless consistent effort has gone in advance.

29

WHY SALES PEOPLE FAIL

One of the main reasons why people fail in the selling profession is because they do not understand the law of averages and hence don't believe in it. The biggest misconception is that business will come to them. In the selling profession, business doesn't come, we have to go out and get it.

Successful people take ownership and accept responsibility. Unsuccessful people end up blaming their luck, horoscope, company, product, manager, customer, the season and what not.

Another Reason for Failure

Not following up in a timely manner makes the individual and organization lose credibility. The key words are 'timely manner.' Too much or too little follow-up is dangerous. For example, if you send a proposal through a courier, then depending on the time estimated for them to receive it, call them 24 to 48 hours after receipt of the courier. Anything too soon might show over-anxiety and anything later may turn a hot lead into a cold one.

The reasons sales people do not follow-up in a timely manner are:

- Non-caring attitude
- Not taking notes
- Not being organized
- Not being goal-oriented
- Laziness
- Thinking that the customer will call if they want to buy
- Over-confidence
- Thinking that after the presentation, the customer will remember them
- Feeling that they are being a pest or too pushy
- Habit of never finishing what they start
- Lying – saying they will follow up without having any intention to do so
- Getting distracted in doing what's easy
- When the time lag is too much they are embarrassed to call

As far back as I can recall, good business leaders and organizations have always felt the need and made the effort to train and educate their sales force.

Many sales people are totally ill-equipped and ill-trained. Customer's needs might have changed over a period of time, but good sales professionals, if trained well, can always enhance the buying experience. Some major reasons for failing in the sales profession are:

- Lack of commitment
- Lack of training
- Lack of monitoring
- Lack of clarity of roles and goals
- Lack of ownership
- Lack of sense of belonging
- Lack of openness
- Lack of transparency
- Lack of coordination
- Lack of team spirit
- Lack of communication
- Lack of proper systems

Many times, sales people fail because the goals have been made unilaterally and without any consideration of resources. A good sales professional should get involved and ask the company to jointly identify the goals and provide the necessary resources to achieve the desired results. Another reason for failure is miscommunication or a lack of coordination – where sales activities do not coordinate with marketing activities.

For example, an advertisement appeared in the newspaper regarding an exhibition to be held in different cities. Due to lack of proper systems, coordination or miscommunication in the organization, nobody in the office knew about the ad till it was released. On that day, phone calls started coming in with people saying. *'I am calling in response to your ad and I want to be an exhibitor in your exhibition.'*

The office staff and receptionist were surprised and asked, *'Which exhibition?'*

What does this example show? Mismanagement results in loss of resources, possibly losing out the money spent on the ad and most important of all, a loss of goodwill.

During my insurance selling career I saw that poor performers had some common behavior patterns:

- They went unprepared for appointments.
- They were not goal-oriented.
- They had no problem in wasting time.
- They indulged in loose talk and gossip.
- They did not practice their sales presentation in advance.
- They never classified their customers as hot, warm and cold.
- They did not evaluate their daily performance. Evaluation helps us to build on the positive and eliminate the negative. Unless you evaluate, how can you know whether what you are doing is right or wrong?

Once a salesperson came back from a meeting where he had gone unprepared. The manager asked, *'Did you get any orders today?'* The salesperson said *'Yes! I got two.'* The manager asked, *'Which ones?'* The salesperson replied, **'Shut up and get out!'**

Carefully observe that all the above reasons for failure are flowing from avoidable self-destructive behavior.

Have a Strong Follow-up

Good sales people differentiate themselves from others by having a strong follow-up system. Timely follow-up builds credibility and trust with the potential costumers. Follow-up is a process which is done pre-sale, during sale and post-sale.

Most sales people are poor at follow-up. A good follow-up takes discipline, commitment and a daily 'To-Do' system.

Follow-ups also include prompt responsiveness by the salesperson. Good follow-up keeps the customer informed and avoids unpleasant surprises. A good salesperson would call the customer to inform him of the status before the customer calls to check. It shows a caring attitude and makes the customer feel important. If the customer is checking the status, he is actually doing the job that the salesperson should have done.

Poor sales people, who don't mean business put the responsibility to follow-up on the customer by saying, 'You can call me or let me know later.'

On the other hand, a good sales professional would accept responsibility by saying, 'If I don't hear from you by . . . I will call you.' If you analyze the above scenario, the first approach was careless where he put himself in the buyer's hands and lost control. In the second situation, the salesman is in charge and remains in the driver's seat.

30

SELF-EVALUATION AND SELF-COMMITMENT

After every sale, evaluate your own presentation and reflect on how you can do better.

What did I do well?

If you want to excel in the profession of selling, evaluate each presentation based on the following parameters. The more honest you are, the more you will get out of this activity. Ask yourself:

- Did I confirm my appointment?
- Did I arrive on time?
- Was my body language confident?
- Was I groomed properly?

* Was I pleasant in my approach?
* Was I friendly without being over-friendly?
* Did I begin with a smile and handshake?
* Did I start the conversation without going off track?
* Were my questions appropriate?
* Did my fact-find uncover the need properly?
* Did I convert all features into benefits for the prospect?
* Did I ask open-ended questions?
* Did I do a trial close?
* Did I handle the objections properly?
* Did I demonstrate good listening?
* Did I close the sale professionally?

Ask yourself, if I were to get a second chance, to repeat this appointment, what would I do differently?

Methods to Increase your Selling Ability

Always ask for the prospect's feedback whenever you fail to close a sale. This approach was very effective for me during my sales career. Here is what I used to say:

'Mr Prospect, obviously, I have not been successful in developing enough confidence in you that we could provide the right solution. I would be grateful if you could tell me what I did wrong, so that I can correct myself in the future.' Invariably, the prospect tells me what turned him off or raised an objection that did not come out before. This sometimes gave me an opportunity to open the door again and possibly make a sale.

After every sales presentation, reflect and evaluate. I remember very distinctly that during my training period, whenever my manager and I came out after making a sales presentation, we would park the car on the side and for the next 5 minutes, dissect the presentation. If my manager made the presentation, he would ask me to evaluate the following:

a) What should I have done that I didn't do?
b) What did I do that I should not have done?

This was a permanent debriefing session to learn from. This practice continued for the first 3 months. Now, imagine making 12 presentations a week for 12 weeks, works out to 144 presentations being evaluated as part of the training. No wonder then that selling skills developed in this way, get internalized and stay with the person for life.

Always get feedback from your existing customers to evaluate your own performance. This kind of evaluation will help you to increase your sales.

Example: A young student was working part-time as a gardener. Once he went to a shop and asked the store owner if he could use his phone. The shopkeeper agreed and the young boy called the lady where he was working and giving a fictitious name said, *'I am EFG from XYZ Garden Maintenance Company, I called to see if I could maintain the garden.'*

The lady said, *'No, I am pretty well taken care of.'*

The boy said, *'Madam, we can do a really good job, better than many.'*

The lady replied, *'I am satisfied with the person who looks after my garden.'*

The boy then came up with; *'We might even do it cheaper and save you some money.'*

The lady said, *'No thanks, the person doing it is just fine. I want to continue to have only him maintain my garden, regardless of incentives.'* The boy thanked her and hung up. It being a small town, almost everyone knew everyone else.

The storekeeper asked this boy why he gave a fictitious name and why he had called the lady who was already his customer.

'You are already maintaining her garden. I have seen you there. I fail to understand why you gave a fictitious name.'

The boy replied, *'I just wanted to make sure that she was genuinely satisfied. If she ever gets a call from a competitor, I know exactly where I stand.'*

What is the moral of this story? This young man checked his grade on customer satisfaction and loyalty. He also evaluated his customer retention grade. This young student, who had never gone through any sales training program, probably knew more about selling and customer loyalty than most so-called sales people.

In the end, success depends on the following 5 Cs and Ts:

1. Commitment   -   Tenacity

2. Clarity   -   Target

3. Character   -   Transparency

4. Competence   -   Talent

5. Consistency   -   Training

Self-evaluation is a process of reflection, leading to learning. Delete the negative you have identified and identify the positives to be reinforced, which will make continuous improvement a way of life.

31

ETHICS

Our credibility determines our profitability, but profitability is not the only reason why we practice values. If profitability is the only reason, then we are only acting, and should go to work in Hollywood or Bollywood. We practice values because we believe in them, and it comes back to the principle that there are things in life that I would do or not do even if no one is watching. It is crucial to remember that **'unethical people bring discredit to everything and everyone associated with them, regardless of their profession.'**

Ethical Benchmarks

A good sales professional must develop his own ethical benchmarks in order to measure the right and wrong. A person may appear honest till tested, because:

- They didn't get an opportunity to cheat so far.
- They are afraid of getting caught.
- Their integrity changes based on the risk and reward ratio. If the rewards are great and the risk is low, they may be dishonest.
- A person may be honest or dishonest based on the stakes that are involved. Someone who may be honest for a hundred dollars or a thousand dollars may become dishonest for a million or more. It shows that integrity is missing and they are ready to sell their conscience based on price.

A good professional makes his conscience and values his guiding principles. Every behavior and transaction is guided by those principles and that becomes his philosophy. His philosophy works as a lighthouse or 'North Star' and helps guide and navigate him in the right direction and towards the right destination. A good professional does not have different moral standards for different situations. In other words, his morality doesn't change from person to person and situation to situation.

Unethical Dealing by Sales People – Cheating the Customer and/or the Company

1. Misrepresentation of facts or misrepresentation of any kind.
2. Offering inducement under the table or giving expensive gifts to influence decisions (bribing).
3. Using company assets for personal use or misuse of company's assets in any form.

4. Theft of data or theft of technology.
5. Adversely affecting the goodwill of the organization.
6. Going out for company business, but doing personal work.
7. Fudging of accounts (padding expense accounts).
8. Giving false sales reports.
9. Concealing facts – not giving pertinent information to the customer. Example: the client feels after the purchase that had he known this information before the purchase, his decision would have been different. This is concealment or cheating.
10. Exaggeration of facts.

There is a world of difference between reputation and character. Reputation is what other people think of us, character is what we know who we are, and they could be two totally different things. That's the difference between doing the right thing for the wrong reason versus doing the right thing for the right reason, e.g., some people are honest because they don't want to get caught while telling lies. They are doing the right thing for the wrong reason. They are only building a reputation of honesty, but the question is, 'Are they really honest?' The answer is, 'No'.

Some people are honest because they believe it is the right thing to do. They are doing the right thing for the right reason, which is called character. Character is what we would do or not do even if we knew we would not get caught or even if no one is watching.

A salesperson has many responsibilities to himself, his family, the organization, customers and the society. A salesperson's obligations are:

1. Economic obligation – In order to honorably discharge his obligation, a salesperson must be economically profitable to himself, his company and to his customer.

2. Legal obligation – Ensuring that he discharges his obligation legally.

3. Moral obligation – He should behave ethically in all his dealings with everyone. Ethical behavior is not a strategy, but a way of life.

4. Social obligation – Ensure that he makes a contribution to society.

Rules to live by:

* Golden rule for the professionals – Treat others the way you want to be treated.

* Golden rule for the unprofessional – Just get the gold, forget the rule or remember that those who have the gold, make the rule.

On a lighter note – Misrepresentation or not? You decide.

Once a life insurance salesman was bragging about his company: 'Our claims department is so efficient that if a man jumps from the 15th floor of our office building, he can collect his claim cheque from the 10th floor, even before he hits the ground.'

Another time, a life insurance salesman was filling out an application for a potential client and there was a question asking the cause of death of his father. The prospect was a little embarrassed because his father had been hanged. The salesman was also uncomfortable writing

> **Moral obligation – A salesperson should behave ethically in all his dealings with everyone. Ethical behavior is not a strategy, but a way of life.**

this cause, so he suggested, 'Why don't we write your father fell down from the platform at a public function?'

Learn When to Walk Away from Business

Remember, relationships are built on win-win principles and not win-lose. In the following situations it is better to walk away from business:

- When the transaction compromises your/your organization's goodwill
- When you are asked to compromise values
- When you are asked to cheat your company
- When the customer is looking at devaluing your product by asking for ridiculous prices
- When the customer's values and your values don't match (The customer suggests that you help him cheat his company, your company, or any third party.)

My experience shows very clearly that the biggest problem-makers are the freeloaders. They want your product by devaluing it with ridiculous pricing and will also be the biggest complainers after the sale. These kinds of buyers or customers will become a pain in future. Remember, the one who wants you to cheat might cheat you on the first opportunity he gets.

Regardless of whether he cheats you or not, would you like to compromise on values to do business?

Once a manager saw in his salesperson's expense account that there was a figure which was very high. He asked his salesperson, *'Can you explain this figure?'*

The salesman said that those were his hotel charges.

The manager said, *'You have to stop buying hotels immediately.'*

Some ethical organizations don't hire people who have worked more than 3 months in an organization – that is known to be unethical because it shows that they consented and approved such unethical practices.

Sales people who lack commitment invariably lie to prospects and give false information. They also lie to their company, making all kinds of excuses as to why they could not make a sale. Only the first lie is difficult to say, after which it becomes progressively easier. Experience shows that people who lie, don't hesitate to steal.

A good professional can never sell anything that deep down in his heart, he doesn't believe in or that goes against his conscience. I recall, once I sold some life insurance where my commission was close to $2,000. I came home but something kept bothering me. My wife could sense it, and she asked me why I was uncomfortable.

I said to her, *'I am not sure I did the right thing and if the client will really benefit from the policy I sold to him.'*

She asked me, *'You know more about the life insurance business than the client does. You also have the facts and information on the financial status of the client. If you want to know whether you did the right thing or not, ask yourself, if you were in place of the client, would you buy the policy? If your conscience says yes, you have earned the commission and can sleep peacefully. But if your conscience hurts you and you have a sleepless night, you know you did the wrong thing. In that case, return the money and cancel the sale.'*

Well, she clarified my ethics. I felt restless and had a sleepless night. Next day, we reversed the transaction and then I felt comfortable even though a couple of thousand dollars meant a lot of money to me at that time of my life. This incident taught me a lesson – integrity and empathy function together, one cannot work without the other. We sell products and services, we sell our professional time – we don't sell our conscience.

A good way to clarify thinking is the rotary four-way test:

- Is it the truth?
- Is it fair to all concerned?
- Will it build goodwill and better friendships?
- Will it be beneficial to all concerned?

Unethical Behavior

When we first hired our computer consultant and maintenance person, he gave us a lot of smooth talk on integrity, good service, quality, reliability and dependability. The moment he got our business we saw his true colors.

Every second day we had a problem as he was stealing information from our office. The experience was a nightmare. He told us he wanted to be a part of purchases or referrals for all items so that he could have a handle on his service. Later on, we came to know that all his referrals had an underhand commission, inbuilt for him, and they padded up the bill by 400%. What was costing $200 was billed at $1,000 with a 25% cut going to the so-called computer consultant. He had given clear instructions to the referrals not to disclose it to us.

Needless to say, the relationship was short-lived and even though we had recourse to sue him, we chose to discontinue our relationship. After he found out that we were aware of his dishonest, underhand dealings he never got on the phone with us.

One of our clients fired his accountant (in my opinion rightly so) for the following reasons:

1. He never kept his appointments.
2. If he was late, he never had the courtesy to inform anybody nor show any remorse.
3. His audits were more of an eyewash than substance and didn't meet industry standards of quality. If he was scrutinized by his own licensing body his license would have been cancelled.

Once, two people died. One was a poor man and the other was a used-car salesman. They both got to the gates of heaven together and at the entrance, the gatekeeper saw their records and said, *'You both have done good things on earth. We were expecting you in heaven and we have permission to grant each of you one wish, anything you wanted in life, you can take it with you to heaven.'*

The poor man said, 'All my life I have been poor, I would like to have a million dollars.' His wish was granted and right away he got a million dollars.

The gatekeeper asked the used-car salesman what his wish was.

He said, *'Just give me a used car and 20 minutes alone with the person you just gave a million dollars to.'* That's it!

The above example appears to be of a fast-talking salesperson who is out to cheat.

Dishonest Selling

An optometrist was teaching his son how to sell. He said, *'If someone comes into your store, let them settle down and then make them try new glasses. Then tactfully appreciate them and convince them of how smart and attractive they look with the new glasses. If they seem convinced, very softly and politely say, $10. If they still seem very pleased, just say "without the lenses". If they ask the cost of the lenses say $10 and if they still appear very pleased, just add the word "each".'*

A young office boy was caught lying and the supervisor said, *'Son, do you realize what happens to those who lie in this organization?'*

The boy said, *'Yes sir, they are all transferred to the sales department.'*

No company in the world can exist without selling. Should selling be perceived as a necessary evil or a respected profession? Some people perceive salesmen as self-serving, manipulative beings. Some sales practices are repulsive and embarrassing, while others are great and rewarding. Selling is a process of convincing others. I cannot think of anything in the world that can be achieved without the power of convincing, whether it is money, friendship or anything. Ethics in sales is no different to ethics in real life. In fact, business has an obligation to stay away from inappropriate or unethical action. Understanding ethics in selling is crucial because selling is something that we all do, all the time, regardless of our status.

It is not necessary that for a salesperson to succeed in his profession, he must be greedy, unethical or materialistic.

Oscar Wilde said, 'Some people know the price of everything, but value of nothing.'

A career in sales has the potential of being a very honorable profession. Unfortunately, unethical sales people succumb to pressure and take shortcuts to make a quick buck. They bring dishonor to themselves, their organizations, families and the profession. Even though the sales profession is driven by short-term rewards of bonuses and commissions, ethical professionals are driven first by integrity and second by commission. Their priorities are clear. They don't trade their integrity for commission. Just like a good doctor makes money by serving the society, similarly a good sales professional serves society and also protects his self-interest.

Giving medicine to the sick is humanity but making people sick just to sell your medicine is inhuman, immoral and unethical. How do the dishonest justify their behavior? What could be the reason for it? Is it that:

* The world is highly competitive – leading to unethical behavior.

- People are looking for short-term gains only – values have been degraded.
- People keep redefining their values, transaction to transaction.
- There is too much individualism.
- Money is the only measure of success.
- Winning at any cost is the only important thing.
- People claim that values are relative. They redefine values to suit themselves.
- If ever they get caught, the remorse is not for 'why did I do wrong?' but 'why did I get caught?'

I feel none of the above are reasons enough to stoop to deception and cheating.

Every profession can justify unethical behavior, e.g.:

- Doctors don't pay attention, because they don't have time.
- Lawyers take dates just to keep billing.
- Teachers have time pressures but that does not justify improper grading of student papers.
- Bumper crops do not justify a farmer using excessive and harmful pesticides.
- Billings are not based on the time spent but how much they can extract.

Which profession does not require dealing with pressures and making value-based choices? Who is not faced with temptation to make extra money or spend more time with the family? We face temptations, both at work and at home, of different kinds and in different directions. Good sales professionals realize that they are not only selling their products or services, but that sales come with a commitment of integrity from all the parties involved. There is a reciprocal relationship between the individual and the organization, sales and service because the actions of one impact the other. Unfortunately, in the real world, unethical practices tend to drive out ethical practices in organizations that are not value based. Where does one pick up unethical behavior? There can be many sources:

- Unethical manager and unethical company culture.
- Parents may not be good role models.
- Unethical messages driven through media and advertising.
- The system that does not integrate ethical practices with sales practices.
- A system that rewards only results, ethical or unethical.

A salesperson was interviewed and asked, *'Do you waste time, come late and gossip at work?'*

The applicant replied, *'No sir, but I am a quick learner.'*

When your actions are in conflict with your values it causes turmoil which is a cause for failure.

EVALUATE YOUR VALUES:

1. Do you conceal valuable information?   YES/NO
2. Do you exaggerate claims about your products?   YES/NO
3. Do you degrade your competitor to make a sale?   YES/NO

4. Do you fudge or cheat on your expense account? YES/NO

5. Would you feel uncomfortable if you are audited item to item? YES/NO

6. Do you feel making a sale is more important than goodwill? YES/NO

7. Do you or your company practice making money by hook or by crook? YES/NO

8. Do you think it okay to make a profit dishonestly when you know you will not get caught? YES/NO

9. Do you think values are subjective and there are no rights or wrongs in life? YES/NO

10. Would you give a bribe or kickbacks to make a sale? YES/NO

If your answer is 'Yes' to any of the above questions, it is just a matter of time before you get into trouble. Don't we face ethical dilemmas every day? Is your conscience a guide or an accomplice? Does your internal voice give you the right direction?

In order to clarify your values, ask yourself the following questions:

1. Who would be hurt by my actions?
2. Would I like someone to treat me this way?
3. Would I be proud of my behavior or actions?
4. Would I rise or fall in my own eyes/esteem?
5. Would my mother be proud of me?
6. Would my children respect me?

7. If my actions become the headlines of the newspaper tomorrow morning, would I like to see my name there?

8. Think – does my action help or hurt me, my family, company or my customer?

Abraham Lincoln came from a poor family and eventually became a very successful practicing attorney. Once a case came to him and after he looked at the facts, he said, *'Technically OK, but ethically not OK. I will not take your case.'*

The man said, *'I am willing to pay your fees.'*

Lincoln said, *'Fees is not the issue, because when I am arguing your case in front of the judge, all the time at the back of my mind I will keep saying to myself: Lincoln you are a liar, Lincoln you are a liar. I cannot live with myself.'*

What Lincoln said in unsaid words is: 'I sell my professional time but not my conscience.'

The above example reinforces my belief that cheats and crooks only learn the tricks but not the trade. They make money at the cost of selling their souls.

A good professional lives by the principles of ethical selling. To him goodwill and conscience are priceless and can never be weighed against money or commissions. Crooks don't mind compromising goodwill for ulterior motives while good professionals would prefer to walk away from business that tarnishes goodwill. **Good sales professionals sell products and services, they sell their professional time but not their conscience.**

AFTERWORD

Some of the greatest leaders in the world like Lincoln, Churchill, and Martin Luther King were also great sales people. They sold their ideas to the world and the masses started supporting them. They spoke from their hearts and not just their mouths. Their words carried weight because their foundations were based on principles of integrity. Hence, their convictions came out as very strong. Because of each one's exceptional selling ability, they created a consensus and changed history for the better.

Principles have existed since eternity.
They were here before we came.
They will be here after we are gone.

If you asked the greatest professionals in the world, how they would describe themselves in one word, that word would be, **'UNSTOPPABLE'**.

This book puts you on the path to being unstoppable.

**BECOME UNSTOPPABLE AND SELL
YOUR WAY TO SUCCESS.**

OPTIMIZE YOUR PERFORMANCE

LEAD successfully · *COMMUNICATE* effectively · *MANAGE* professionally
Based on *VALUES & ETHICS by attending the following*

BLUEPRINT FOR SUCCESS (3 Day Workshop)
GROW BY CREATING NEW LEADERSHIP AT EVERY LEVEL
ACHIEVE EXCELLENCE BY MANAGING DIFFERENTLY

MASTER SELLING SKILLS (1 Day Workshop)
OUTSELL YOUR COMPETITION BY MASTERING SELLING SKILLS

PUBLIC SPEAKING (2 Days Workshop)
MASTER PLAT FORM SKILLS BY LEARNING THE ART OF PUBLIC
SPEAKING

COMMUNICATIONS (1 Day Workshop)
COMMUNICATE WITH CLARITY AND CONFIDENCE
BUILD BRIDGES THROUGH EFFECTIVE COMMUNICATION

TIME MANGEMENT (½ Day Workshop)
   a. ACCOMPLISH MORE, IN LESS TIME
   b. TAKE CHARGE OF YOUR LIFE

CULTURE CHANGE PROGRAM (31 DAYS CULTURE CHANGE PROGRAM)
Inject new vitality and create a culture of trust and accountability,

POSITIVE PARENTING (1 Day Workshop)
GOOD UPBRINGING MAY GIVE HEADACHES, BUT BAD UPBRINGING
ALWAYS BRINGS HEARTACHES.

MOTIVATIONAL PRODUCTS
   - See – Overleaf

Enquire about public and in-house programs from:

Qualified Learning Systems
C-6/4, Vasant Vihar, New Delhi – 110057, **India**
Tel: + 91-11-26148804
Fax: + 91-11-26149658/26142656
Email: shivkhera@shivkhera.com

Associate offices:
144 North Beverwyck Road,
 #349, Lake Hiawatha, New Jersey 07034, **USA.**
Fax:(973) 3357030

124, Tanjong Rhu Road,
Casuarina Cove,# 06-06, **Singapore** - 436916
Tel.: (65) 63481954
Fax: (65) 63424921

Please send me information on

- The seminar 'Blueprint for Success'
- Keynote presentations
- In- house seminars
- Public seminars
- Audio and video products
- Books
- Bulk purchases
- Other motivational products

Name_____Title_____
Company_____
Address_____
City_____State_____Pin_____
Telephone (off)_____Fax_____

Visit us at: www.shivkhera.com